ROOSEVELT

SARGENT'S PORTRAIT OF ROOSEVELT

ROOSEVELT

His Mind in Action

BY

LEWIS EINSTEIN

BOSTON AND NEW YORK
HOUGHTON MIFFLIN COMPANY
The Riverside Press Cambridge
1930

The Riverside Press
CAMBRIDGE · MASSACHUSETTS
PRINTED IN THE U.S.A.

E

PREFACE

It is customary to speak of Roosevelt as a typical American and he would have desired to appear before history in this light. If devotion to America, if belief in the future of America, if ambition to serve the country by leading it to greatness, means being a typical American, no one has ever better deserved the title. Popular opinion which attaches this designation to any leader of whom it feels proud offers the soundest test. Yet, seen from another angle, there was little typically American in Roosevelt. Though he abhorred the word, his beginnings were those of a dilettante and his early career was eminently that of an amateur. He took up law and dropped it, he took up politics and dropped it, he took up ranching and dropped it. Sometimes his experience led to failure; at others to success if success be measured not in its immediate but in its ultimate meaning. Until the White House loomed before him, Roosevelt's primary purpose was to train his own personality toward an end still undefined.

He never passed through the hard battle of upward struggle which has characterized the early life of most American public men. The dangers to which he exposed himself were greater, the hardships may have been more severe than those of the vast majority, but they were voluntarily sought after, and did not form part of his normal or necessary pursuits. He was totally unlike the mass of his countrymen, either in their education, their occupation, or in their ideas. No American and no modern has resembled more the great men of the sixteenth century in their desire for a well-rounded life of thought and action, in their thirst for the varied experience offered by learning and adventure, and in their wish for fame. He, too, felt the ambition to attain an all-round accomplishment and proved by his career that the Renaissance ideal was large enough, and still vital enough, to find fulfillment in the broad sphere of American industrial democracy even better than in the narrow atmosphere of a petty Italian court.

Words cannot convey the impression which quickened whoever came near Roosevelt to retain through life the influence he emanated. A foreign ambassador once told the writer how he himself became conscious of this influence years later, when, walking in a lonely mountain valley close to the Lake of Geneva, he had reached a narrow and dangerous ledge. He was alone at the time and there was no reason why he should proceed any farther, for he realized that if he were to fall down the steep precipice underneath, he would not be found till long afterward. But the feeling that Roosevelt under similar circumstances would have gone ahead also made him persevere. The spirit still marched on.

This book is only an attempt to penetrate into the mind of Roosevelt, to try to discern the springs of his action and watch him darting through the pages of American history which he so notably enriched. Motives cannot always be weighed nor the eternal equation solved between self-interest and national

interest. Yet one may seek to follow the personality
of the man through the varied incidents of a career
rich in experience, commanding in leadership, and
touching near to the great questions which at a critical moment affected the United States.

Roosevelt stands large enough to be represented as
he really lived and not to be portrayed solely radiant
in Olympian sunlight without any of the shadows cast
by his human form.

> 'Speak of me as I am, nothing extenuate,
> Nor set down aught in malice.'

Impressions are largely personal, and those which
weight the finer scales of judgment can never be read
alike. The Nation's instinct, summing up greatness in
a few general words, has rightly consecrated his fame
as an American hero. For those who feel this and
cherish his memory in lasting affection, yet seek to
penetrate below the surface to detect the swirl underneath, perhaps these pages may offer some appeal.

The writer desires gratefully to acknowledge the
kindness of Chief Justice Charles E. Hughes, the
Honorable Lucius N. Littauer, the Honorable Homer
Cummings, and Major W. W. Hicks, United States
Army, in reading over certain sections of his manu-
script and giving him the benefit of their suggestions.
In no way, however, are they to be regarded as re-
sponsible for any of the opinions he has expressed.

CONTENTS

ILLUSTRATIONS

ROOSEVELT

His Mind in Action

.·.

CHAPTER I

STRUGGLE

I

THERE is a brownstone house on Twentieth Street in New York just east of Broadway. Fifty years ago it was the appropriate residence for a wealthy New-Yorker. Thirty years ago it was still typical of thousands of similar houses which in serried rows of dull ugliness then lined the streets on either side of Fifth Avenue. To-day, surrounded and overshadowed between tall business buildings, it stands alone as a curious vestige from another age which already seems remote. The house which witnessed the birth of a giant appears a dwarf.

In this house Theodore Roosevelt was born on October 27, 1858. On his father's side, for two centuries, his family had been associated with New York, enjoying standing in the community without any of its members ever attaining even the eminence of mediocrity. The search for inherited traits in the case of great men is always interesting and nearly always baffling. None of the seven generations of Roosevelts who had lived on the island of Manhattan offer any real clue to the personality of the future President. Nay, more. Theodore Roosevelt spoke with the highest admiration of his father. He describes him as the best and bravest man he ever knew and draws his portrait in words of the most loving sympathy. His father, who was a strong Lincoln man, lived through the period of our Civil War without ever participating in the struggle. If he felt the duty to enlist, if he was restrained by his Southern wife, or by family obligations, remains unknown. But when the Spanish War broke out, Roosevelt wrote that he did not wish ever to have to explain to his children why he did not take part in it.

It is difficult to understand either Roosevelt's character or his genius by searching among the obscure figures of his forbears. Yet the influence these exercised on his later life cannot be dismissed so easily. He was fond of referring to the different strains of blood in his veins. Blood in the United States, it is true, has of late years acquired fresh significance, or rather a reversion to an almost primitive meaning. In Europe, ancestral pride usually attaches itself more narrowly to the possession of landed property or the perpetuation of a title or historic name through generations. In America, the strain of blood is referred to in a far wider sense which embraces vast aggregates of the population and the significance of which is out of all proportion to more spiritual and evolutionary considerations. When Roosevelt refers to his Dutch, his Irish, his Scottish, and his German ancestors, he does this in no sense from the pride of birth, but rather with the wish to identify himself more closely with millions of his fellow citizens who share similar strains. He relates that his first American ancestor, Klaes Martensen Van Roosevelt, came to New Amsterdam in 1644 as a 'settler.' Half humorously, half with the same purpose, he describes this designation as 'the euphemistic name for an immigrant who came over in the steerage of a sailing ship in the seventeenth century instead of the steerage of a steamer in the nineteenth century.'

Roosevelt intended to imply that his own ancestors were of the same hardy stocks as those who have built up the great foundations of the United States. He does not try to attach his lineage to origins of real or fancied Old-World greatness. His own pride, his intelligence, and his political sense never for a moment lent countenance to such a thought. He suggests instead that his family rose from small beginnings, prospered through sturdy virtues, and that as the descendant of such ancestors he himself typified the growth of America.

Yet few families could be less typical of that growth than the Roosevelts. Far from possessing the hardy adventurous spirit of the pioneer, or those frontier virtues which he was never tired of exalting, far from even repeating the history of so many American families from their origin as small farmers, for seven generations from father to son, every Roosevelt was born and had lived as merchants on Manhattan Island. If any of them ever went West or sought adventure, the future President, so careful to point out facts of such a nature, has failed to chronicle this.

His identification with the race history of America
is therefore in a physical sense largely apocryphal.
This in no way challenges its essential truthfulness.
The modern historical outlook, which lays so much
stress on economics and so-called race, tends to
neglect the more spiritual aspects of human development. Insufficient account is taken of change through
environment or the fact that men tend to become
what they are of their own volition. Nations have
never been formed out of one blood, but have been
knit together by common pride and common memories and the resolution, conscious or otherwise, to
work out their future problems together. As the
pedestal on which to rest his fame, Roosevelt desired
and strove to be the typical American. Like a great
river swollen by many small tributaries, he wished to
feel, and even more to make others feel, that he was
what he was because of his own diverse origins and experiences which formed part of our national history.

On his mother's side, Roosevelt could find better
justification for such fancies. Her brothers had been
Confederate naval officers, one of whom built the
famous Alabama. Among all the members of his
family only 'Uncle Jimmie' Bulloch can be said to
have attained any distinction as a fighting man.
Perhaps he inherited a further characteristic from
him. After the Civil War, this uncle, whom he describes as another Colonel Newcome, settled in
Liverpool to become a die-hard Tory and acquire a
particular aversion to Mr. Gladstone. His nephew relates that he sincerely believed Gladstone to have
been a 'man of quite exceptional and nameless in-

famy.' Roosevelt also, later in life, was not reluctant to expressing strong opinions about his enemies. He was less able to understand the strong opinions his enemies expressed about him. But when people believed unjust things to his detriment, he consoled himself by thinking of Uncle Jimmie Bulloch's conviction regarding Gladstone.

Roosevelt's Southern blood gave better justification to a broader national origin than he could derive from the Knickerbocker strain. It allowed him, in a more personal way than would otherwise have been possible, to associate the South in his appeal. No President before him had been so national in his outlook. Although at times he ruffled white susceptibilities by his attitude toward the Negroes, the South felt pride in his achievement even when it withheld from him its vote.

There was another pride of family in Roosevelt, the keener because it always remained unmentioned and silent. He found cause for satisfaction in descending from seven generations of New-Yorkers who had enjoyed high consideration in their community. The standing of the older families in America from an original small eminence has been derived, at least in part, invisibly by immigrant and other pressure from below, which, as it rose in the scale, pushed always higher those who had been there before them. In a vast expanding city of multiple origin like New York, which had grown out of the smallest beginnings, the prestige of a continent was cast, far beyond their deserts, on a few families who had maintained a position since the city's early days. The consciousness of this distinction, the feeling that there was no one in America superior to him in lineage, and that this fact was recognized generally wherever he went, was born in Roosevelt and sunk deep into his soul. Few could better justify such a conviction, although good taste and political wisdom left it unexpressed through life. He was too much of an aristocrat ever to exult in his aristocracy, and too much of a politician not to realize that the only unforgivable sin in American politics is condescension.

It is no easy matter to force the description of any man's character into the mold of words, and that of Roosevelt, which on its surface seems rugged, forceful, and impulsive, remains underneath subtle, intricate, and elusive. The stress Roosevelt laid on his many friends in obscure and humble walks of life, scattered far and wide through the land, arose in part from his own pride of birth. His democracy was conscious and deliberate. It sprang from the wish to find elements of broad sympathy and common interest in his fellow citizens. In Maine or in Dakota, on the railroads or in the slums, he met men with whom he could play or work, fight or reason. He made friends with the trapper from the North Woods, the Western sheriff, the railway fireman, the Russian Jewish boy from the East Side whom he appointed a policeman. The pleasure he found in their society was real. It was the pleasure of a man filled, to a degree never surpassed, with the true sense of life and with the love of doing. Of a man with a great vision of America, a belief in the reality of its mission, and who found in the diverse elements of its composition

the human material with which to accomplish his
ideal. His democracy was not that of Lincoln swap-
ping stories with his neighbors. It was not the democracy of millions of his fellow citizens. Yet it was
no less sincere because its origin was different, or
because it emanated from his own convinced superiority. Hidden pride might precede it, ambition
might enter into its essence, but the ultimate goal
before him was always to arouse in an American
way those virtues which make for a nation's greatness.

II

Few have ever written more charmingly of their
childhood than Theodore Roosevelt. The pages of
his 'Autobiography' which he devotes to his early
days are unsurpassed in their picture of happy family
life, related with humanity and delicacy. He has
drawn portraits of his parents and of his Aunt Anna
with an affection which must always endear them to
lovers of children. Roosevelt was then a delicate and
sickly boy who suffered much from asthma. There
was in fact nothing Spartan in his bringing-up and
nothing remarkable in his precocity. Least of all was
his early education typically American. He never
went to public school, but was taken to Europe, for
which at the age of ten he entertained a most profound contempt, characteristic of that arch-conserva-
tive *chauvin*, the American small boy. He acquired
an early interest in natural history and, like countless
other lads of his age, began a collection of curios
which he styled a museum. He read the usual boys'

books of adventure and delighted in Mayne Reid and Captain Marryat.

If one side in Roosevelt's youthful education stands out, it is his love of natural history, which lasted through life. Nearly all children are interested in birds and animals, but few take lessons in taxidermy at thirteen, or go so far as to make collections of birds as he did a year later in Egypt and in Palestine. Beyond this, if he felt any glimmer of ambition, he is careful not to mention the fact. Few American boys escape from the wish to be President at some future moment of their lives, and it would not be surprising if young Roosevelt had also experienced this ambition. If so he is careful not to indicate the hope. His 'Autobiography,' it is true, was published in 1913, when Roosevelt was fifty-five years of age. The recollections of his boyhood are, however, extraordinarily vivid and precise, with a wealth of detail which not many men could conjure up after so long an interval. If he left out from the story of his life all mention of hopes of a nature to evoke a smile, such reticence affords only another indication of his sense of humor, for no American boy can admit his dream of the future Presidency except when standing by a cut cherry tree.

There exists another reason why Roosevelt was unwilling to convey, even by suggestion, the impression of having been an early prodigy. Although few men have ever possessed more spectacular instincts, few also have been more simple in certain expressions of their life. Nor was such simplicity altogether unconnected with design. In after life Roosevelt

spoke of himself as a man possessed of only average
attainments which he had been able to raise entirely
by application and force of will. In his 'Autobiography,' intentionally he laid stress on his own mediocrity as a shot and as a rider, and his merely reaching
a level of performance which lay within the power of
any average man. In dwelling on the ordinary
nature of his aptitudes, his purpose is to associate
himself by suggestion with the unexpressed ambitions
of most Americans. A skill too great as a horseman or
a shot would have separated him from the mass of his
countrymen and widened those chasms of difference
which inwardly he remained deeply conscious of, and
which he was always trying to bridge over. He
realized that, as a child, his education and experience
had not been that of the ordinary American boy.
With real art, he points out that his tastes were yet
the same, and that his early years were spent in pursuits within reach of the average child.

At the age of fifteen he was sent to a private school
in New York. Such schools served to acquire famil-
iarity with a dull routine primarily intended to prepare for entering the colleges. Studies were designed
with this goal in view, and possessed little ulterior
purpose. In general, no attempt was made to awaken
the intellectual curiosity of boys, to grasp their individuality and guide their mental formation for
some other end than examinations. Certain of the
teachers displayed an almost obsequious respect for
the wealth of their pupils' families. It was said of a
schoolmaster mentioned by Roosevelt that he once
pointed to four boys with the remark that between

them they represented a hundred million dollars. Men familiar with the stodgy materialism of New York in those days, against which Roosevelt later revolted, will better appreciate the significance of this remark.

Boys are by nature conservative. Especially those who attend the schools of the wealthy and have not the prospect of sharp struggle before them feel little interest in the ferment of ideas and gratify their energy mainly with games. Roosevelt relates that he came to school with a very one-sided training. He was strong in French and German, in history, geography, and science, but lamentably weak in mathematics, Latin, and Greek. Teaching in these branches was mainly out of textbooks and usually aided by the pupils' use of cribs. Sound training in the classics was rarely acquired, and it was not surprising that, for a boy so receptive as young Roosevelt, the private school made little impression. His schoolmaster, Arthur Cutler, later dwelt mainly upon the energy and vivacity he displayed and his ability to add up a long column of figures more rapidly than any boy who had ever come under his guidance.

Whether college life was also as negative as his 'Autobiography' suggests is more questionable. Roosevelt valued his Harvard connection for itself, but also for the reason that he valued every connection which extended his roots and increased his influence. On occasion he spoke feelingly in after years of college friendships and of the benefit he had derived from these, singling out one man in particular to whose advice he had always listened with advantage in his

political career. He felt at home with university
friends, and many years afterward, returning from
his triumphal journey when he had been welcomed by
the sovereigns of Europe, he could jest with old-time
intimates about his experiences with kings in a way
which never reached the public ear. If he slurs over
the time passed at Harvard, if he fails to mention his
companions, the reason may be found in one of the
purposes underlying his 'Autobiography,' which he
designed as a document to place him before the
American people and enshrine him for posterity in
the manner in which he wished to appear.

To the extent that Harvard represented an élite,
intellectual or social, to the degree that it cut him off
from the broad life of America, he passed lightly over
its influence in the chapter on his education. Yet no
President ever prized learning more than Roosevelt,
or appreciated more the importance of cultivation in
enriching American life. But as a man he did not care
to show that even in his early years he was affected
by the restricting influences which prevailed in an
academic atmosphere. His comment about the
instruction he received at Harvard is that, while
genuinely democratic in one way, it was not so
democratic in another. Too great stress was laid on
the development of the individual, and but slight
attention given to pointing out that individual's
duties in life toward his fellow citizens. Roosevelt, of
course, was writing from his outlook in 1913 and was
not attempting to retrace the story of his years at
Harvard except in so far as this might serve to agree
with his later theories.

The university curriculum was then far narrower than it has since become. Scholarship and science, at the time, were alike under German inspiration and meticulously thorough in the study of details, whether of the laboratory or in the text. This spirit of work, which was justified as a reaction against the superficial generalization of former college education, was always alien to Roosevelt, who was no specialist. He wished to connect science and learning with life, and loved nature in the open air and not when viewed as tissues under the microscope. Educationally he found on looking back that Harvard had done little for him. He made this remark with some pleasure, although generously appearing to blame himself for not deriving more benefit from his instructors.

His own ambition, at this time, was to become a scientific man of the type of Audubon. During his college years he had as yet no intention of going into public life and neither studied elocution nor practiced debating. His activity, however, was already extraordinary in its variety, but somewhat indiscriminate. He taught Sunday School for three and a half years and then resigned rather than join the Episcopalian Church. He preached morality and high purpose to those he met. He gave opera parties, attracted attention by driving a dogcart, and took a four-in-hand with friends to spend the day in the country shooting at glass balls. He went in for light-weight boxing and despite his frail body attempted to overcome those with whom he could not cope. This personal side of his years at Cambridge he fails entirely to chronicle. Neither then nor later does he mention men of his own standing in the Porcellian Club, some of whom were always to remain his closest friends. Is this due to the reticence of good taste? Is it the wish to hide the more intimate aspects of his life whenever these do not serve a public purpose? May there not be another reason which made him desire to keep in the background all sides of his activity which were of a nature to separate him from the mass? In letters to his sister written as an undergraduate he mentions how much he enjoyed the fashionable life of Boston. When he went West to shoot birds just after his graduation, he wrote from the farm where he stayed: 'The farm people are pretty rough, but I like them very much; like all rural Americans they are intensely independent; and indeed I don't wonder at their thinking us their equals, for we are dressed about as badly as mortals could be.'[1]

Roosevelt impressed his classmates at college with an undue consciousness of his own social standing. There was an assumption of personal superiority on his part which he tried to establish in every phase of his conduct. So long as this was admitted, and just so long, his intercourse was easy and cordial. At a Harvard reunion years afterward, when a former classmate repeated certain comments made about him, he remarked with feeling that his old companions had always refused to acknowledge this superiority. Yet in his 'Autobiography' he implies that he was neither very clever nor very studious, merely a 'reasonably good student.' Again comes out his later wish to be one of that great average which forms our body politic and whose leadership he still hoped to regain. For in the innermost recesses of his soul he knew in 1913, when his 'Autobiography' appeared, just as he had known thirty-five years before at Harvard, that he did not belong to that average and had never formed part of it. And there are those alive to-day who still recall him as an undergraduate exclaiming that he wanted the admiration of his fellow men.

III

A great deal of ill-considered nonsense has been written by misguided admirers of Roosevelt as a kind of world specialist like Faust, exploring the depths of all human endeavor with a perfection in his versatility which raised him to eminence in every field. Roosevelt would have been the first to deplore such praise if he had not been amused, for no one cherished a keener sense of the absurd. The excellence of his French or the merit of his scholarship were never the virtues which made for his real greatness and his sense of humor lent no countenance to such a picture. On the contrary, as he grew in fame he tried to convey the suggestion of his own mediocrity. After he had achieved the highest honors that man can covet, he spoke disparagingly of his aptitudes in sport and intellect. Roosevelt's belittling estimate of his capacities is in certain respects no more accurate than the extravagance of his most uncritical admirer. In part such disparagement was based on pride, in part it was not without political design. Written many years later, when the episodes of his varied career had shaped themselves very differently in their

light and shade, his eminence as a public man made
unnecessary any pride in minor achievements. That
he would willingly have accepted such inferiority in
his youth was more questionable.

After his graduation, he hunted on Long Island and
went on shooting expeditions to Maine and to the
Rockies. The pursuit of sport was for him the shaping
of a natural instinct. His early weakness as an
asthmatic boy had long been outgrown. The vigor of
life ran lustily through his veins to seek outlet in the
work of the body. And the exercise of his muscles by
contributing to the quest for experience in every field
of effort enlarged his own feeling of mastery.

Roosevelt left Harvard with wide rather than with
deep interests. His father had died during his sopho-
more year and he had inherited a competence which
relieved him from the necessity of bread-winning.
He married a Miss Lee, of Boston, whom he had met
as an undergraduate. Though he looked for occupation, studied law, and continued his historical writing,
little was henceforth heard of his early wish to become a scientist. As a vocation science appeared too
narrow for his own wider interests. Yet always he
retained his fondness for natural history, though
later associating this with a taste for sport and
adventure in the wilds.

Roosevelt's career from the time he left Harvard
was really an education in sympathy. The average
college man of his standing, imbued with the prejudices acquired by training and surroundings, is apt
to look down on others less fortunate and assume
superiority by a feeling of contempt. Roosevelt was

not free from such prejudices, for he never lacked tl
consciousness of his own importance. His merit, at
time when higher ambitions could only have appeare
as remote dreams, lay in overcoming such inhibition
By cutting loose from their narrowness, he felt broa
enough to find underneath the common elemen
which brought him into touch with his fellow mei
The spark of revelation Keats first found on lookin
into Homer, Roosevelt discovered on taking up di,
trict politics.

His early contact with the smaller political worl
familiarized him with life in a way from which he wa
later to profit. New York City politics were bot
highly specialized and little elevating. It is amon
the paradoxes of American municipal governmen
that the noble ideals written into our charters bea
but slight relation to reality. Yet the spirit of cit
politics also presented certain redeeming sides whic
he was discerning enough to detect. Of jobbery an
corruption there was plenty. But accompanyin
these ran a current of human sympathy.

In his 'Autobiography' he has recounted his earl
political experiences with vividness and humor. H
made friends with district leaders and relished thei
companionship; he canvassed for votes and enjoye
his campaign. His more enthusiastic biographer
have tended to magnify this portion of his career as i
it contained already the premonition of later genius
Its real significance is not what he did to distric
politics, but what these did for him. They were onl
the opening chapter of political education in the lif
of a man who always welcomed experience for it

own sake, and who to his dying day remained young
enough at heart to enjoy its varying phases. In later
years these early episodes appeared to shape themselves in a way which led up to the well-rounded education of a great public man. But all this was still
premature. The early steps in his career were not the
conscious design of any ultimate plan, but only an expression of interest in public affairs and the ability to
treasure its lessons.

Far more than is commonly realized Roosevelt then
learned from Tammany Hall. It remains a paradox
that the man who stands preëminently for having
brought a great moral element into our politics and
for having reformed public life should have taken his
first lessons in the human side of politics from the
most notorious organization in our political world.
But Roosevelt had penetrated into the reason of
Tammany's hold on the masses in New York, and
distinguished the good from the bad. In its essence
Tammany Hall was a feudal structure built around
lieges and vassals who afforded each other protection
and service, often for nefarious purposes. Later,
Roosevelt aptly compared its one-time leader, 'Big
Tim' Sullivan, in his principles and actions, to a
Norman baron in the years succeeding the Battle of
Hastings, applying eleventh-century theories to nine-
teenth-century democratic municipal conditions.

Roosevelt understood the secret of Tammany success. The organization could survive a dozen defeats
and a hundred attacks because even its corruption
was built on a human basis. From top to bottom
there prevailed a personal contact of friendship and of

service. Its leaders looked after the interests of those under them, irrespective of who they were. If a poor man needed a job, he would find one with the street-cleaning force or in city traction. If he was temporarily in want, he would be helped out of his difficulties. Assistance was given without regard to politics, and in all personal matters even a political adversary would receive every courtesy. A system such as this, built up by the effort of many years of patient service, explains the power of Tammany. Its enemies could at times fasten gross scandals on its conduct of affairs and before the weight of the shame it would sink to defeat only to rise again.

Tammany taught Roosevelt the value of the personal element in politics. Loyalty was inspired, not by the civic reformer's cold ideas of abstract virtue, but by the warm human touch. Men followed a chief, not because his life was elevating, but because they felt something in him which responded to their own sympathies. Henceforth, Roosevelt deliberately began to build up that vast personal following which marked him as the greatest of popular leaders. Henceforth, from small beginnings, little by little, he laid the foundation of a great structure of men and ideas, which he identified with himself and made peculiarly his own, till a compliment by Roosevelt attached to him his man, in the same way as a word addressed by Napoleon to a soldier of the Old Guard.

Tammany taught still another great lesson to Roosevelt. His instincts, his training, his environment and associates would normally have led him to

the cause of reform in politics. But his contact with
Tammany showed him the weakness of the good government movement and why it had never succeeded
for any length of time. Reform in New York was inclined to be as spasmodic as it was frigid in its stern
virtue. Emanating from the top, it never took hold of
the masses nor attempted to understand their wants.
Loud in indignation before elections, after these were
over, it remained quiescent, with interest confined to
a few enthusiasts. Reformers lacked the organization
of Tammany, lacked the tradition of Tammany,
lacked the warmth and human sympathy of Tammany, in which lay the real secret of its success.

In later years Roosevelt took pride in calling himself a 'practical idealist.' He found his idealism in the
planks of reformers. Then, as afterward, he borrowed
these unstintedly, adapting them so that they became his own. Early experience, however, made him
realize his inability to promote such measures so long
as he confined his ways to those of so-called cranks.
It gave him, too, a kind of contempt for these, the
contempt which the man of action has for the vision-
ary who is unable to carry out his ideas. Instead he
felt real respect for an organization like Tammany,
with its brawn, its punch, and its good-nature. He
could forgive many things, but never the weakness of
inefficiency. Later he quoted approvingly the remark
made by a Governor of Texas that he might pardon
a man who had tried to shoot him, but never one who
had shot him accidentally.

IV

Roosevelt's entrance into politics was made in what is still known as a 'silk-stocking' district, long after such words have ceased to convey their former connotations of luxury. Many years later this district was described to the writer as 'the greatest and wealthiest Assembly district in the world.' But wealth concerned itself with professional politics only at a more elevated stage and Roosevelt found himself warned by his friends, as many others have been warned before and since, against the low nature of politics, which were controlled by office-holders, saloon-keepers, and men who were not gentlemen.

The most significant feature of this district was the fact that it contained little or no mean between the two extremes of its inhabitants. Its leading residents were men, in certain instances, of national importance: capitalists, bankers, lawyers, or railroad magnates, whose investments were as broad as the United States and who were unduly inclined to identify national interests with their own. Outside an exceptional few they left 'peanut politics' to the professional politicians, having neither the time nor the inclination to concern themselves with what they regarded as a degrading pursuit. The professional was usually a man whose occupation in life was bound up with the technical details of the organization of the political machine in its varying aspects of preparing nominations, elections, appointments, and legislation. A wide rift existed between the politicians and the solid business men inhabiting the brownstone houses then characteristic of the best residential

quarters in New York. Roosevelt realized that between Tammany and Republican politicians there was
less difference than between the Republican politicians and the people these represented. The system was one which suited both sides. The politicians
obtained a livelihood built on their ability to control
the avenues of legislative power. They asked the
residents of the brownstone houses only for sub-
scriptions and votes at election times. The large
contributors offered their benefactions principally to
allow the politicians to run the machinery of vote-
getting, in order afterward to influence legislation for
selfish purposes. They gave liberally for office-
holders to be subservient. Beyond this existed no
intercourse. Most of the brownstone-front people
were perfectly satisfied to be left alone, and only
spasmodically felt any concern in the cause of civic
welfare. Their complacent assumption of superiority
based on wealth and standing remained content to
leave what seemed like the pickings of power to
smaller men whose activity they despised.

Roosevelt's merit is to have realized the anomaly
of so ill-balanced a situation and to have tried to
remedy the travesty of popular government which resulted from this abuse. By his family, his upbringing,
and his associations, he belonged to what were known
as the 'classes.' But patricians have often become
leaders of the masses since the Gracchi perished in
their struggle two thousand years ago. Roosevelt's
entrance into district politics was, however, a greater
innovation in the New York of the early eighties than
the Roman precedent. The smug materialism of that

period was still unaccustomed to a spectacle of this
nature, and Roosevelt derived no little enjoyment
from its novelty. District politics into which he
threw himself afforded him the exercise of still undeveloped tastes which had not found their outlet.
He felt genuinely attracted by the goal of civic virtue,
by the tactics to obtain this which involved a fight
with the unrighteous, by his visits to saloon-keepers
and local bosses, by the astonishment of his own class
at his procedure, and the astonishment of the politicians that one of his class should descend into their
arena. All this delighted him. Above all, the opportunity for acquiring new experience was welcome.
No one ever took more pleasure in the novelty of
knowledge, whether from books or from life, and
Roosevelt's later journey to the headwaters of the
Amazon was not so daring in its exploration as his
first descent into the district politics of New York.

His mentor was Joe Murray, an Irishman who had
left Tammany Hall because of some slight, who was
ambitious to become leader of his district, and who
brought to the Republican organization a knowledge
of Tammany methods of real value. Roosevelt
describes him in glowing, if somewhat excessive,
terms as being 'as straight a man, as fearless, and as
stanchly loyal' as any one whom he had ever met. A
feeling of warm friendship grew up between the two,
the first and also the most important of many friendships which all through life Roosevelt made with
men of the people. It is a tradition of our politics that
those who hold real power usually stay behind the
scenes and rarely seek office for themselves. Joe

Murray, who understood the different elements com-
posing the district, saw that Roosevelt's connections
made him an available candidate for the Assembly
nomination. Rightly he picked him out to win. In
his campaign Roosevelt displayed the energetic enthusiasm which later made him famous, but 'it was
not my fight, it was Joe's; and it was to him that I
owe my entry into politics. I had at that time neither
the reputation nor the ability to have won the nomination for myself.' So Roosevelt wrote, years later,
in his 'Autobiography.' The most powerful man of
his generation exulted in the fact that he owed his introduction to American politics to the favor of an
Irish machine politician.

The political talent possessed by Roosevelt must
sooner or later have discovered itself. But the friendship of Joe Murray also taught the future President
what organization meant and gave him a wholesome
respect for the 'machine.' Henceforth, whether
utilizing its influence or fighting it, he always understood its value. He learned, also, at this stage, the
worth of personal friendship in politics, especially
with those who could never be his rivals. He became
familiar with the mosaic of different origin and
condition which forms the electorate of our great
cities, and thereafter on many occasions he was to
utilize his accurate knowledge of this. Always preaching the goal of an Americanism which knew neither
creed nor race nor birth, he acquired the politician's
eye to distinctions of this nature, if only to appear to
disregard them. He wrote in this spirit that it was no
small help in making himself a good citizen and a

good American that the political associate with
whom he was on the most intimate terms during his
early years was 'a man born in Ireland, by creed a
Catholic, with Joe Murray's upbringing.' With no
less admiration he speaks of Arthur von Briesen, who
embodied the spirit of the German idealists of '48,
and of Jacob Riis, whom, although born in Denmark,
'I am tempted to call the best American I ever knew.'

The Legislature in Albany, where he served for
three years from 1882 to 1885, offered further
opportunity for his political education. He felt at
first like 'a boy in a strange school.' If the Assembly
district which had elected him was unlike any other
district in the State, he himself was unlike any other
Assemblyman. He started by facing the criticism of
ridicule which awaited him before that of misrepresentation had begun. His mutton-chop whiskers, his
drawl, his alleged Harvard manner lent themselves to
easy caricature. A contemporary squib that

> 'His strong point is his bank account,
> His weak point is his head,'

seems a vulgar absurdity in the light of history. But
he was then an unknown quantity, and perhaps his
most signal performance during his three terms in the
Assembly was in raising the status of the amateur in
politics.

The Legislature at Albany, with the varying interests it provided, the hopes it aroused, and even the
disappointments of failure, proved for Roosevelt an
admirable training-school of experience. Corruption
and integrity were interwoven far more intimately

than the onlooker could suspect and it was not always an easy task to unravel their threads.

The Republican State organization was then entirely under the control of Tom Platt, who fathered the selection of legislators, contributed money to their campaign, and after their election dictated practically every step they took at Albany, assisting them even in their petty local interests in return for their subordination to his purposes, which were primarily the continuance of his own power. Platt was personally honest, but he found nothing amiss in taking contributions, which formed the basis of his authority, from the large corporate interests which required legislative favors in return.

At Albany, Roosevelt distinguished himself by his violent attack on the unholy methods of this system, made possible by the domination of the machine. His efforts were seldom effective in obtaining remedial legislation, but he did much to check corruption and bring about cleaner administration. He tried unsuccessfully to impeach a judge. He incurred the enmity of the powerful Elevated Railway of New York by opposing a measure designed to relieve it of half the burden of its taxes. He attacked 'the infernal thieves and conscienceless swindlers who have had the Elevated in charge... with their hired newspaper, with their corruption of the judiciary, and with their corruption of past legislatures.[2] He aroused the most bitter animosity and came in for equally strong praise and condemnation.

In making his fight, Roosevelt was not infrequently the isolated figure which he afterward be-

came. Occasionally he would work with his party
organization, which paid him the compliment of
selecting him as its candidate for Speaker when he
had no chance of success, only to drop him as soon as
its members formed the majority. More often he
relied on chance allies, picked up even among his
adversaries. Hardly ever, then or later, was he able
to feel the phalanx of the party machine behind him.
He made mistakes. He had risen too quickly, and
when he became leader of the minority, he proceeded,
in his own words, 'to lose my perspective, and the
result was that I came an awful cropper and had to
pick myself up after learning by bitter experience the
lesson that I was not all-important and that I had to
take account of many different elements in life. It
took me fully a year before I got back the position
I had lost.' [3] His difficulty was partly due to a temperament which was too individual to accommodate
itself within the mediocrity of the organization. Also
to the instinctive feeling, then still in its infancy, that
the roots of his strength were drawn from the people
and that his mission lay in making himself the spokes-
man of their interests.

At Albany his closest friend for the three years he
served in the Legislature was Billy O'Neill, who kept
a small crossroads store in the Adirondacks. 'In
most other countries,' he wrote, 'two men of as
different antecedents, ancestry, and surroundings as
Billy O'Neill and I would have had far more difficulty
in coming together.' Again one discerns the pride of
birth, the satisfaction at being able to overcome its
appearance in order to remove the causes of separa-

tion from his fellow Assemblymen and the tendency
to attribute the merit for this to American democracy.
He felt a little latent admiration for himself at his
readiness to sink all distinctions. He and O'Neill
stood together, he tells us, in every legislative fight.
Their views were similar and they looked at things
from the same angle. Yet Billy O'Neill has gone down
to oblivion and his name lives only in Roosevelt's
pages. Fortune never favored him, and the future
President, looking back over his own vicissitudes, remarks that any man who has attained distinction, if
he will be frank with himself, must admit that
Chance is a big element in success.

V

The wish for popular appeal made Roosevelt in
later years cultivate arts of publicity with a reward
attained by few. But this side of his talent had hardly
revealed itself at Albany and only at times was he able
to arouse indignation against the measures he had
pilloried. He fixed the blame for this in the supine-
ness of public opinion in the choice of its representa-
tives. Years afterward, the writer recalls Roosevelt
in his office at 'The Outlook' commenting on how the
voters of a State may at the same time elect a corrupt
Legislature and an upright Governor, yet will punish
the latter for failing to block the corruption of the
Legislature for whom they themselves have voted.
However illogical this seems, the reason is that the
public takes merely a spasmodic interest in politics.
Men are unable to continue long at high tension.
They remain indifferent over the smaller offices and

opinion becomes exacting only with the dignity of the post. The average American neither knows nor cares much about the character of the lower officials for whom his vote is cast until this is obtruded unpleasantly on his attention.

As Assemblyman, Roosevelt exhibited on a smaller scale the sympathy for the under dog and contempt for self-approving wealth which later he displayed as President. The main lines of his character had set early in life, and years afterward the domestic policies which made him famous in the White House were largely the expansion of what he tried to do at Albany. Traits which later made him the idol of millions of Americans, in his youth were still regarded as eccentricities. Yet Assemblyman Roosevelt in the early eighties was not a very different person from President Roosevelt. With age he was to acquire more experience, more executive ability, and to know America far better. But inherently he was the same man. More than he, it was the country which had changed in its receptiveness, and he, by act, pen, and word of mouth, assiduously over a long period of years, was instrumental in bringing about this change. His later evolution was one of power and punch rather than of breadth and idea. Broad he always was, for his cultivation was genuine and his origin and education gave him a certain detachment hidden by the very force of his presentation. The originality of his achievement at this time was to have coupled such detachment with an intensely practical outlook on the nature of politics.

Early days at Albany gave no indication of the

promise of his later career. Roosevelt received praise
and made some but not an extraordinary impression.
He took interest in measures of good government, and
what later became known as social welfare. The
activities of the farmers, or the needs of small towns,
occupied him less than the problems of the great city
and the housing of the working class, which awakened
his true sympathy. He was appointed member of a
committee of three to investigate conditions in the
tenements and see if legislation was required to prohibit cigars being manufactured in these. He saw the
work of cigar making carried on by men, women, and
children, eating, living, and sleeping in the same
room — at times two families in one room. A bill to
prohibit this had passed the Legislature, but had been
declared unconstitutional by the Court of Appeals,
where the Judges denounced the law as an assault
upon the 'hallowed' influence of 'home.' Roosevelt
writes that this case first roused him 'to a dim and
partial understanding of the fact that the courts
were not necessarily the best judges of what should be
done to better social and industrial conditions. The
judges who rendered this decision were well-meaning
men. They knew nothing whatever of tenement-
house conditions! They knew nothing whatever of
the needs, or of the life and labor, of three fourths of
their fellow citizens in great cities. They knew
legalism but not life.' [4]

The later Roosevelt wrote these words, but the
earlier Roosevelt also felt that something was wrong
in this decision of the Court of Appeals. The feeling
burrowed in his mind till it overcame the influence

of the atmosphere in which he had been educated, for like most Americans he had been brought up to hold the courts in special reverence as bulwarks against demagogic legislation. He relates that it took more than one experience to shake him out of this attitude.

This remark is partly an apology and partly a profession of faith. In his later career Roosevelt was deeply stirred by what appeared to him as class justice. It is also true that, looking back on the earlier chapters of his life, he found in the tenement cigar case the first example of his interest in social welfare. Roosevelt possessed an extraordinarily retentive memory and many years later his recollection of this case still loomed fresh in his mind. He found in it the precedent for his interest in the welfare of the masses and his criticism of the courts. The extraordinary feature is that this criticism lay silent and was not followed by any other perceptible expression before well-nigh thirty years had passed.

It is also curious that after the long period of waiting that he had to endure, recognition should have coincided with the reawakening of the same interests which he had felt while in the Legislature and which in the interval had remained largely dormant. Why was there this hiatus? How is it possible to explain the long lapse of time which intervened between his attack on the corrupt interests at Albany and his indictment when President against malefactors of great wealth?

No explanation advanced is entirely satisfactory, but an analogy drawn from the experience of his later years may throw some light. Roosevelt's family life, as is well known, was eminently happy. His affections were deep and he felt intensely the love of his home. Yet to carry out his journey to Africa and his later explorations in Brazil, he did not hesitate to leave home and family over a long period of time and to incur danger without any convincing reason. In Central Africa, as in the Brazilian jungle, his days were intensely occupied by varied pursuits. There is no indication that he missed his home, nor would the reasoned philosophy of his conduct have allowed him to admit this.

If this is true of Roosevelt in his private life, how much truer is it of the man in his public capacity. He could take up a cause and invest it at once with the fierce ardor of an intense conviction. He would make it his own and attach to it the loyal devotion and enthusiasm of others who recognized the power of his leadership even when they mistook the exclusiveness of his interest. At Albany for the first time he had come into contact with problems of property, of life and law. He threw himself into the struggle with the generosity of a bountiful nature. But as soon as he no longer felt personal responsibility in handling these problems, his interest at once became focused in other pressing directions. Questions of labor and of capital were relegated to the vast reservoir of facts and theories kept by him in reserve. Active interest was gone, not to be revived again until the same responsibilities confronted him, when at the top of the ladder, that he had encountered on its lowest rung twenty years earlier. The essential unity of his character shows itself in the fact that his reactions to the same problems should have been identical in spite of the lapse of so long a time.

After he had aroused expectations and ambition at Albany which were still imperfectly satisfied, he retired from politics for reasons, certain of which are not clear, though grief over his wife's death contributed to shape his decision. He withdrew at the time when he seemed nearest to success, almost as suddenly as he had entered. His career at Albany had given him prominence and enlisted the highest praise from such men as Joseph H. Choate and the press of the country in general. He had demonstrated his power of leadership and had secured enough following among the younger element to enable him early in 1884 to defeat the Platt organization for the selection of delegates to the Republican Presidential Convention. His reputation had already spread through the country, and when he arrived at Chicago he was looked up to as a young leader of promise and was able to take a fairly effective part. Roosevelt bitterly fought Blaine's candidacy, but supported him, after some hesitation, when he became the choice of the Convention, for reasons disappointing to some of the more intransigent reformers, who expected him to bolt. After the Convention, he wrote to his sister, Mrs. Cowles: 'I suppose all of our friends the unco good are as angry as ever with me. They had best not express their discontent to my face unless they wish to hear very plain English. I am sorry my political career should be over; but after all it makes very little difference.' [5]

Politics had been his first adventure. He had
ntered public life partly for the sake of experience,
artly as a reformer, and at first, perhaps, because he
elt pleasure in witnessing the astonishment of his
riends. He had touched new interests, but had fallen
etween two stools, for he was whole-heartedly
either with the reformers nor with the machine.
Ie was by himself, isolated, with a small following,
ut without the support to go ahead. Already, after
is first election to the Assembly, he had written to
friend, 'Don't think I am going to go into politics
fter this year, for I am not.' At that time he was
tudying law and writing a 'History of the Naval
Var of 1812.' Yet twice he allowed himself to be
enominated and reëlected. In 1883 he bought a
anch on the prairies. His interest in the law had
lways been feeble. In politics he had made insuffi-
ient headway. The West attracted him and his
olitical interest diminished. Again the amateur in
im spoke almost unconsciously. He had had his fun,
e had acquired experience; now he wanted some-
hing new.

VI

'I rode fifteen miles last night, the thermometer
eing twenty degrees below zero, bringing in a buck
fter missing two others. My cattle are looking well
— and in fact the statesman (?) of the past has been
nerged, alas, I fear for good, into the cowboy of the
resent.'

So Roosevelt wrote to his new friend Lodge from
is newly bought Western ranch. He had known

Lodge very slightly when at Harvard, and it was only
in the spring of 1884 that politics brought them to
gether and kept them intimately together in a life
long friendship. 'Dear Mr. Lodge' soon became
'Dear Lodge,' speedily to change again to 'Dear
Cabot.' A similarity of origin and of education; a
cultivated interest in life and in the amenities of life
a fondness for American history, and, in their early
days, for riding; above all, a real taste for practica
politics made for this friendship. Roosevelt found in
Lodge what no man in New York could then offer
him, the combination of the gentleman who was a
the same time a scholar, a sportsman, and a politi
cian. From the time they were brought together by
a common opposition to Blaine, which they felt as
reformers, and a common determination to suppor
Blaine when nominated, which they felt as practica
politicians, Lodge became Roosevelt's closest friend
personally and politically. Soon Roosevelt wrote
him with words of praise which in later years he
lavished so bountifully, 'I do not know a man in the
country whose future I regard as so promising as is
yours.'

The legend of Roosevelt retiring from the brilliant
promise of his legislative career in order to take up
ranching is only partly correct. In 1883 he had
acquired two cattle ranches in the Bad Lands of
Dakota. He tried to develop these as an investment
but without great success, and brought to assist him
two friends from the Maine Woods. He has de
scribed, with rare charm, his life as a ranchman, in his
letters, in his 'Autobiography,' and in two of his

THEODORE ROOSEVELT
On the round-up, 1885

books. The freedom of the West appealed to him. He enjoyed the open air, the life on the plains, his hunting expeditions, and the adventures he encountered. The frontier was then not yet a thing of the past. Roosevelt found pleasure in his friendship for 'Hell-Roaring' Bill Jones and other cowboys and sheriffs of his kind. He felt the same satisfaction as on his first entrance into district politics, when thinking of the astonishment of the folks at home. Again he was seeking new experience, amid surroundings which appealed to his real love for sport and adventure, and his wish to justify these tastes in a less unproductive way than merely as a hunter. He was frankly delighted with his broad sombrero, his fringed and beaded buckskin shirt, his horse-hide riding-trousers, braided bridle and silver spurs, and he dwells on his preference for this kit to riding after an anise-seed bag, dressed in a red coat. There is the same intense pleasure at what he is doing and the same satisfaction also in letting his friends know of his achievements.

His mercurial temperament swayed as usual between depression and elation at his future prospects. When trouble with Mexico seemed possible, he wrote at once to offer to raise some companies of horse riflemen. 'I haven't the least idea there will be any trouble; but as my chance of doing everything in the future worth doing seems to grow continually smaller, I intend to grasp at every opportunity that turns up. I think there is some good fighting stuff among these harum-scarum rough-riders out here.' Ten days later,[6] he again writes to Lodge: 'I wrote as regards

Mexico *qua* cowboy not *qua* statesman.... If a war had come, I would truly have had behind me as utterly reckless a set of desperadoes as ever sat in the saddle.'

All this time he read and wrote. Roosevelt was no natural stylist and his literary task meant labor. 'Writing is horribly hard work to me; and I make slow progress.... My style is very rough and I do not like a certain lack of *sequitur* that I do not seem to be able to get rid of.[7] His 'Life' of Benton was the fruit of this effort — a spasmodically written biography, with a few brilliant chapters, mainly about his beloved West, opinions forcibly expressed about foreign policy, and reflections on the opportunity we had lost forty years earlier, of a war with England which would then have left us in possession of the entire Pacific Coast. There are many tedious pages in this book, which was written by Roosevelt without real interest. He was conscious of the imperfections, due also to remoteness from library facilities, and evolved the book, as he humorously wrote to Lodge,[8] mainly out of his inner consciousness. With his 'Winning of the West,' designed as his great work, he hoped to do better and avoid the roughness in style of the 'Benton.' Yet he was not altogether dissatisfied with the latter, and declared characteristically that it had not been written 'to please those political and literary hermaphrodites, the Mugwumps.'

His heart was not in biography, but in the West, which thrilled him with its promise of adventure and of empire. In the vast expanse of the prairie he found

the attractions which delighted him from his boyhood
to his dying day. He had watched the buffalo grazing
and enjoyed the wild life of beasts. He had seen man
with his primitive instinct. The hunter's quest, life
in the open air, with books, and guns, and horses,
with chosen comrades on whom he could rely, and
who accepted his leadership without reservation —
appealed to his taste and wish for hardihood. He, the
city man, found satisfaction in discovering that his
courage was no less than that of the rough characters
among whom he lived. He was proud of his ability to
understand the cowboy point of view, to associate on
a footing of what seemed to him equality, and to feel
common elements between them. In his whole life
Roosevelt's receptive nature always found sympathy
for every American save only those of the class from
whom he sprang. The smug, wealthy business man,
comfortable in the conviction of his virtuous superiority, was the only American type which remained
instinctively repellent to his nature.

In the West, also, Roosevelt discovered the promise of America. As an historian, he read aright the
significance in our national growth of the Western
migration of the race. As a statesman, he foresaw the
splendor of the great empire whose foundations were
being laid. The spectacle of the many-sided West
thrilled him. It developed his character and taught
him to suppress if not to forget early assumptions of
social superiority. His life on the plains developed
his native manliness and made him feel henceforth
that his roots were as much in the West as in the
East. His sympathetic understanding enabled him

to grasp this feeling and gave him inner satisfactions which helped to round out his personality in the sense of a wider Americanism.

His experience, none the less, was still that of the amateur. Although he took his full part in the round-up and was in the saddle eighteen hours of the day, although he caught cattle thieves and displayed high courage in the achievement, the volume of Matthew Arnold in his pocket on that famous adventure offers the most convincing proof that he was in the West but not of the West. The cowboys liked him, but no cowboy ever mistook him for one of their own. He did not mistake himself. In his heart of hearts he remained what he was. The physical circumstances of his life meant only the alternation of experience.

Read his letter to his sister, Mrs. Cowles, written from Medora, his Dakota ranch, on April 22, 1886:

'The Janviers must be very pleasant and I hope they will turn out desirable additions to our limited list of "intellectual" acquaintances and further material for that distant salon wherein we are to gather society men who take part in politics, literature, and art, and politicians, authors, and artists whose bringing up and personal habits do not disqualify them for society.... Why is it that even such of our friends as do things that sound interesting do them in a way that makes them very dull?'

Roosevelt the ranchman out on the Western plains was dreaming of his future life in New York. He was even dreaming of New York politics. He was back at Sagamore Hill in the fall of 1885, when, for a time, he joined the red-coated hunters and broke his arm jumping. He was back again a year later to accept a hopeless nomination for Mayor of New York.

VII

Roosevelt entered the Mayoralty contest of 1886 in New York with no illusions. He had accepted the nomination, as he then wrote Lodge, with the most genuine reluctance, as the contest was hopeless from the start. A political career was again fixed in his mind. He had just obtained a local success at the primaries, and his national reputation was spreading, for he had been asked to take part that year in the Maine and the Ohio campaigns. His reluctance to be a candidate for Mayor of New York did not arise from the fear of defeat, which was a foregone conclusion, but from the dread of not making a good enough campaign. 'If I make a good run it will not hurt me; but it will if I make a bad one, as is very likely.'[9] He did not want a damaging defeat which would ruin his future chances. 'In all probability this campaign means my final definite retirement as an available candidate; but at least I have a better party standing than ever before, and my position there is assured.'[10] Time and again in his career this fear of failure in public life preyed on his mind. Roosevelt's buoyant exuberance and the confidence which impressed people were only veils hiding the doubt and depression often gnawing his soul, the secret of which he unbared only to his intimates.

The Mayoralty fight was then three-cornered, for Henry George had come from the West to run on a

socialistic platform. His radicalism alarmed many
voters, normally friendly to Roosevelt, into sup-
porting Abram G. Hewitt, a Democrat of high
character nominated by Tammany. Roosevelt threw
himself impetuously into the campaign and made a
'rattling canvass.' He polled over sixty thousand
votes, yet came out only third best. Roosevelt's defeat was a disappointment and seemed even worse
than he feared. He blamed for it the people of his
own class who lived in the brownstone fronts, and
who, alarmed by a socialist, preferred to vote for the
representative of Tammany. The 'timid good,' as he
contemptuously called them, were for Hewitt. 'The
better element have acted with unscrupulous mean-
ness and a low partisan dishonesty and untruthful-
ness which would disgrace the veriest machine heelers.
May Providence in due season give me a chance to get
even with some of them!' he wrote to Lodge on the
eve of the election. [11] Depressed by the failure of his
efforts, he felt disappointed with politics, resentful
and angry with the people of his own class, and
especially distrustful of himself. To his sister, Mrs.
Cowles, he wrote, two months later, from Florence:
'I don't much care whether I change my residence
from New York or not. I have not the slightest
belief in my having any political future.' [12]

Immediately after his defeat, he had sailed for
England to marry Miss Edith Carow, whom he had
known since his boyhood. The happiness of his mar-
riage, the interest of his travels in Italy, and the
hearty welcome he found among English friends soon
distracted his attention. He thoroughly enjoyed his

stay in London. He followed the debates in Parliament. He met politicians who were also men of letters, and men of letters who were also politicians, like Bryce, and Morley, and Trevelyan, with whom he formed a lifelong friendship. He was put down at the Athenæum and dined and lunched every day and had 'countless invitations to go down into the country and hunt or shoot.' He went to stay with Lord North in 'a really first-class English country house.' He hunted in Essex and the Shires, and though he found the jumping less stiff than on Long Island, the hunt required greater headwork. He had a 'lovely time' and met the 'very pleasantest people.'[13]

Sport in England, life in England, and the talk of the cultivated circles he frequented gave Roosevelt an acute pleasure, though not as ends in themselves. He felt among British friends a more congenial atmosphere and environment than he had ever experienced among the people of his own standing in New York. The tastes of the latter were not his tastes, and he knew that his personality even when respected was regarded by his New York friends as wayward and eccentric. In England he found greater consideration for individuality, and a readier sympathy with his own fondness for sport and letters, politics and adventure. He could enjoy the social side of British life with far more pleasure than he took in the same order in America. The English country and the amenities of intercourse appealed to certain pleasure-loving and cultivated tastes which were deep-rooted in Roosevelt.

He contrasted this with all he most disliked in the

smug, opulent, dull respectability which characterized New York in the eighties. His money-making
instinct was never strong, and the sense of its de-
ficiency made him all the more intolerant of the faults
of those at home who measured success in life by its
self-approving standards. He had suffered and was
destined to suffer, if not from actual lack of means, at
least from the inability to live easily according to the
standards of his taste. Even on his honeymoon he
had written to his sister that the expenses at Sagamore Hill would have to be cut down to the lowest
possible point. There was some question of his selling
the house, but this he had not the heart to do.[14] And
all this time people whom he knew in New York, and
whom he despised for their vulgar outlook, were immeasurably richer than he, and freed from all such
miserable anxieties.

With the British it was otherwise. Sport was relieved by love for the soil and money-making was not
the sole purpose of existence. But in his soul he knew
that the land was not his land, the people not his people, and even the social intercourse he had enjoyed, by
making him more conscious of the difference between
the two countries, attached him more deeply to
America. The cultivated conversation, the round
of varied pleasures which appealed to his taste in
England, were only, so to speak, the outer fringe of
his own personality. He heard within him a half-
conscious call toward something deeper which he
knew was there, though he could hardly as yet
define its nature. His anti-Anglomania, as he dubbed
it, was an expression of this instinct. It reflected his

aversion to Americans of his own class who, when
they were not intent on money-making, were striving
to copy Englishmen in their sports. He felt a collec-
tive contempt for the Long Island red-coated hunting
crowd, although ready enough to find individual
friends among them. Until he had discovered his
real opportunity at home, this antipathy provided
a defensive protection for himself against taking undue pleasure in the gratification of similar tastes.

He knew that the fulfillment of his own career
could only come through America. But the circumstances of his life gave as yet small promise of a future.
His years in the Assembly at Albany had led to very
little. He had fought a forlorn fight in one National
Convention, which had resulted in estranging from
him many of his former supporters. He had run last
in the race for Mayor and had come out of this with
fresh grudges and renewed distrust in his own
future. Even his Western venture was turning out
a failure. A month after he had been enjoying life in
London, he wrote to Lodge from his Medora ranch
that the cattle business had gone through a crisis,
and 'the losses are crippling. For the first time I have
been utterly unable to enjoy a visit to my ranch.
I shall be glad to get home.'[15]   And home was Sagamore Hill, where he spent the next two years.

VIII

The two years passed almost uneventfully. Roosevelt hunted occasionally, visited his Western ranch,
and continued his historical writing. For the time
this seemed to satisfy him. He felt that he was doing

honest work, that he was occupied creditably, and he professed to be philosophical about political success or failure. 'It often amuses me when I indirectly hear that I am supposed to be harboring secret and bitter regret for my political career, when as a matter of fact I have hardly even when alone given two thoughts to it since it closed, and have been quite as much wrapped up in hunting, ranching, and book-making as I ever was in politics.'[16]

After his 'Life' of Benton he had begun a biography of 'that entertaining scamp' Gouverneur Morris, for the American Statesmen Series. The eighteenth-century atmosphere in which Morris moved was little congenial to Roosevelt. The conversation of Paris salons and the graces of Old-World life seemed to him to lack fresh air, and he preferred the boastful un-couthness of Benton's Western associates to the refinements of Versailles. √He worked hard on his 'Winning of the West.' Again he made up his mind that he would go in 'especially for literature, simply taking the part in politics that a decent man should.' This resolution went the way of many others. Public life irresistibly attracted him. 'I would like above all things to go into politics; but in this part of the State that seems impossible, especially with such a number of very wealthy competitors.'[17]

He made speeches whenever he had the chance, neglected no opportunity to express himself publicly on every topic, lashed the Mugwumps with fine vituperation and called their favorite journalist 'a malignant and dishonest liar.' Many of the traits he exhibited as President were already in evidence. The vigorous expression of his opinions, the directness of his statements, the moral emphasis of his point of view, had crystallized in their mold. Years only gave him more experience and a higher power of expression, but substantially he always remained the same man.

Already he was expressing hope that the Republican Party should steer clear of becoming a party of reaction. He talked a great deal about the tariff, and though he could be emphatic, he was never able to summon up much genuine enthusiasm for its merits. He accepted it because the Republicans and the country were definitely committed to a policy of protection, and any sudden reversal of this would be unwise. But in his opinion it was equally so to announce that under no circumstances must the tariff be touched and that every other issue was to be subordinated to it. In reality the schedules of protective duties failed to interest him, and belonged to an order far too material for his sympathy. Roosevelt did not object to their purpose, but he could not work himself up to any degree of conviction about their inherent virtue, and preserved what he dubbed 'a tinge of economic agnosticism.' Writing to Mrs. Cowles during the Harrison campaign,[18] he said: 'I really take very little interest in what people regard as the main issue; our nation covers a continent and there are fifty questions of more lasting importance to us than either free-trade or protection — questions such as the liquor laws, ballot reform, the civil service.'

Civil service reform had always attracted him.

The abuse of patronage for selfish and partisan purposes has been the plague of our governmental
methods. American political life is both as highly
specialized as it is elemental, with something of an
open gap between which leaves a weakness in our
system. Men with long training and men with no
training almost haphazardly fill the same political
offices, without the public finding interest enough
generally to distinguish the difference in the character
of their tenure. The country has been slow to recognize the viciousness of doling out offices high or low
as rewards for political service in money or kind. The
small efficiency return in many of our public affairs,
in contrast to that developed by private business, and
the harsh treatment often meted out to officials of
ability and devotion, have been only a part of the
price paid for the continuation of these abuses. The
reformer in Roosevelt revolted at a system which had
nothing to commend it and has since to some extent
been corrected in its lower levels. 'The Administration's record on Civil Service Reform is disgraceful,'
he wrote to Lodge.[19]

When Harrison became President, Lodge tried
unsuccessfully to secure for Roosevelt the appointment of Assistant Secretary of State. He would
have been glad to accept this or almost any office
which might give him the promise of useful occupation. It did not take long for him to realize that his
failure to obtain the post was a blessing in disguise,
for he could have done nothing in such a position.
The State Department has never lent itself readily
to reformers, and Roosevelt had shown himself too

OUR NEW WATCHMAN — ROOSEVELT

violent in his previous fight against Blaine to accept
the latter's leadership gracefully. Every office filled
by Harrison was keenly scanned by Roosevelt and
called from him some expression of opinion. 'I do
hope the President will appoint good Civil Service
Commissioners,' he wrote Lodge. In May, 1889,
President Harrison named Roosevelt a Civil Service
Commissioner at a salary of $3500 a year. For the
next six years he served as a member of this Commission.

This was his first Federal post, and in his 'Autobiography' he has described his work with humor and
given an admirable account of the real meaning of
the spoils system in our politics. As Civil Service
Commissioner, he assumed national duties for the
first time and obtained an experience which later was
to prove invaluable. He soon prided himself with
cause that he had made the Commission a living force,
and, so long as he was responsible for the law, 'it
should be enforced up to the handle *everywhere*;
fearlessly and honestly.' He was willing to be turned
out, legislated out, 'but while in I mean business.'

Roosevelt injected his vitality into the performance
of duties which proved as varied as were his own
interests. The texts of executive orders placing under
civil service regulations classes of minor Federal
Employees provide as dull reading as anything in the
world. But to carry out such orders meant in every
instance a real fight, as the patronage these were
intended to curtail formed the groundwork of the
politician's power.

Laymen are often astonished by the paucity of

administrative enactments and the limited scope of executive orders. They expect greater results from the labor of the mountain and fail to appreciate the violent combat which every forward stride inevitably arouses. In such contests interest is derived far more from the clash of opposite forces amid troubled atmospheric conditions, which remain unrecorded, than from a result which appears at times to be almost negligible. In his many struggles for civil service reform, Roosevelt fought on the side of the angels. 'Now I have been a real force and think I have helped the cause of good government and of the party,' he wrote to Lodge.[20] All he had to do, as he remarked, was to enforce the law, and enforce it he did with a vigor which the law had never before known. In picturesque language he described the men he ran up against: 'Cleveland's postmaster at Milwaukee is about as thorough-paced a scoundrel as I ever saw — an oily-gammon, church-going specimen. We gave him a neat hoist,' he wrote to Lodge.[21] Nothing afforded him more pleasure than to pit himself against some Senatorial Ozymandias who, in the past, had been accustomed to override the official regulations roughshod. The combative instinct, always strong in Roosevelt, would then be aroused. He felt himself struggling for a cause which, unlike tariff or currency, really appealed to him by its complex of human interest and its identification with good government. At last he was handling affairs which concerned the Nation at large and was able to feel satisfaction for the punch he could put into his work.

The criticism he met with, the bitterness of the denunciations against civil service reform, the violence of the attacks made personally against him, provided an intense gratification. A double-page cartoon which appeared at this time in 'Puck' paraphrases an incident which had occurred when the explorer Stanley navigated the first steamboat up the Congo and the natives ran along the banks yelling with rage and striving to check his progress with primitive weapons. In this cartoon Roosevelt is represented on the deck of the Civil Service Reform Monitor, while from the river-bank Platt and Quay, Wanamaker and Dana, dressed like African savages, throw spears ineffectually against him.

The opposition of the politicians was the best reward he could obtain. It made him stand out as the champion of a good cause and this placed him in a welcome light before the people. He was associated in their minds with practical reform. His name became better known nationally, and all over America thousands of men heard of his work and began to look up to him as a reformer. To offset this, he alienated many of the politicians, and aroused violent animosities, which also retarded his advance. Without angling for the support of the machine, but without disdaining this, his political instinct went deeper even in these early stages of his career. He knew that his overwhelming personality would never long be able to adjust itself within the narrow framework of a party organization, and his unshaped hope lay in the discovery that the farmers in the country and the men in the small cities cherished a vague dislike for a boss and a queer distrust of the machine, which was 'a real marked attitude of the Republican Party.'[22]   To capture the confidence of the farmers and small people and make himself their leader meant success, though anything short of this spelled failure. Roosevelt was digging in richer earth than surface politics. Ungrateful as the soil then seemed, when later his time came, the rapid spread of his popularity was in no small degree due to the fact that its seeds had been sown during his term as Civil Service Commissioner.

His work in Washington benefited him for after years in another way. It familiarized him with the social side of the capital and he made a personal acquaintance with the leaders in our national life which led to many warm friendships. The politician whose elevation to the Presidency has followed roads which have kept him at a distance from Washington may easily find himself, when in the White House, isolated and handicapped by an imperfect knowledge of men which comes from an absence of earlier personal relations which he no longer is able to take up on a footing of equality. Roosevelt's apprenticeship as Commissioner served him in good stead. He soon felt more at home in the capital than in New York. The social side with its political background appealed to him more than the life of his native city.

'Washington is just a big village, but it is a very pleasant big village. Edith and I meet just the people we like to see.... We dine out three or four times a week and have people to dinner once or twice.... The people we meet are mostly those who stand high in the political world and who are therefore interested in the same subjects that interest us; while there are enough also who are men of letters and of science to give a pleasant and needed variety. ... It is pleasant to meet people from whom one really gets something; people from all over the Union, with different pasts and varying interests, trained, able, powerful men, though often narrow-minded enough.' [23]

George Washington would never have written such a letter. Lincoln could never have written it. It is Roosevelt all through, with his expectant, wide-awake interest, his eminently social tastes in the best sense of the word, his keen intellectual curiosity, and the pleasure he always found in the exchange of ideas. There is still something unconsciously of the eighteenth century in the breadth of Roosevelt's cultivation, in his sympathy for every manifestation of human endeavor, in his real fondness for the polite tradition even when he appeared farthest from this, and also in his aloofness from commercialism. He hated the boring stodginess of the brownstone fronts which he had left behind in New York.

'I never can like and never will like to be intimate with that enormous proportion of sentient beings who are respectable but dull. It is a waste of time. I will work with them or for them; but for pleasure and instruction I go elsewhere.' [24]

There was another reason which made him like Washington. Life, especially in those days, was on a simpler scale in the national capital than in New York, and Roosevelt did not feel handicapped to the same extent by his modest means. He was able to gratify his eminently hospitable instincts and offer his guests California claret at twenty-five cents a bottle without fatal results, as he jocosely wrote. He enjoyed thoroughly the life he led and the companionship of his intimates — Lodge and Henry Adams, John Hay and Tom Reed and the Wolcotts, and 'Springy' and Speck, the future British and German ambassadors — how much he preferred the talk of these men to social life in New York! His delight was unceasing in the variety of his own experiences, political, literary, and sporting, each in its little world, complete in itself, and each world profoundly ignorant of the other. Roosevelt brimmed over with pleasure in the consciousness of this varied life which he and Lodge could enjoy and chat over together, but which was sealed to so many of their friends who remained confined within their narrow groove.

As Civil Service Commissioner, Roosevelt had done good work. But he soon realized that he had spent his slender influence with the party. His pace had been too rapid, his voice too loud. President Harrison refused to consider the changes which Roosevelt proposed to him and the latter left the White House disgruntled. 'He won't see us or consider any method for improving the service.... It is horribly disheartening to work under such a Chief.' [25] The feeling came over him, which was to recur continually in his life, that he had reached the end of his career. Although Cleveland reappointed him as Commissioner, his task was no easier. 'I am personally in such a tangle of animosity with Carlisle and Hoke Smith that I may have to go at any moment.' [26] He wrote to his sister, 'I do not see any element of permanence or chance of permanent work for me in the kind of life where I really think I could do most.'

Again came doubts about the wisdom of seeking Government service and the belief that he must go back to his former writing. Money matters also were troubling him, for he had overrun his income. Everything would have to be done to cut down expenses or Sagamore must be sacrificed, and this was likely to happen anyway when the children began to be educated. He summed up the situation in another letter to his sister: 'The trouble is that my career has been a very pleasant, honorable, and useful career for a man of means; but not the right career for a man without the means.' [27]

IX

'Colonel' Strong, the new Mayor of New York, elected on a ticket of reform, offered Roosevelt the position of Police Commissioner, which he accepted after some hesitation, urged by his brother-in-law Douglas Robinson and by Senator Lodge. The new post meant leaving Washington after six happy years. It also meant the probable neglect of his literary occupations. He had accomplished all he could hope for as Civil Service Commissioner. He did not wish to remain indefinitely in a minor position in the capital and political ambition made it advisable to be identified once more with his native city. To continue to reside in Washington either as Civil Service Commissioner or in some similar appointive position seemed like digging into an honorable inertia which responded little to the overflow of energy pent up within him.

Roosevelt would probably have been puzzled to say whether the appointment as Police Commissioner meant a step forward in his career or otherwise. His original hesitation to accept the post indicated the doubt existing in his mind. He would be obliged to leave national for local affairs, to turn his back on the close neighborhood of great questions discussed from a comfortable berth amid agreeable surroundings, with friends high in the country's councils. Instead he would be forced to take up the petty intricacies of the city police, with all their sordid details, their paltry ambitions, and their background of corruption. It was not an alluring exchange and to make this no small resolution was required.

The first letter he wrote to Lodge from the Police Department in New York assured the latter that there was no fear of his losing interest in national politics. The new job, in his mind, was to be only temporary. In a couple of years he expected to finish the work with the police and be ready to take up something fresh. If nothing else offered, he would then remain in New York. He was aware that the great prizes of America do not go to men living away from their roots. The ease of life in Washington unfits many a man for the rougher struggle in his own community. It is not difficult to lose touch with the soil, and soil in American politics means life amid surroundings with which one has been identified for years, often to incur only jealousy, defeat, and disillusion.

At first, Roosevelt threw himself into the new duties with his customary energy. He found these absorbingly interesting, as he always found every task he undertook in life. 'I have never worked harder,' he wrote to his sister, Mrs. Cowles. 'I have the most important and the most corrupt department in New York on my hands. I shall speedily assail some of the ablest, shrewdest men in this city, who will be fighting for their lives, and I know well how hard the task ahead of me is. Yet in spite of the nervous strain and worry, I am glad I undertook it; for it is a man's work.' [28]

The Police Department gave Roosevelt opportunity for personal touch of the kind he most enjoyed. On top he found the system bad and its methods corrupt. Below, the human material was splendid and the personnel under him was manly and courageous. Here was a job after his own heart. It brought him into touch with the masses in that variegated medley of races which goes to make up the proletariat of New York. He approached these with sympathy, which in turn awakened confidence and aroused enthusiasm. Responsibilities of office brought out the best in Roosevelt. The sincere interest he felt in his work, his broad understanding and tolerance, contributed to shape before him an ideal of Americanism and good citizenship which he delighted to preach. The Police Department was a little world in itself, but in close touch with the greater world of the metropolis. Its duties brought the force into daily contact with crime, vice, and politics. The tendency to be lax or venal could only be arrested by discipline and pride of service. Roosevelt was admirable in this task. He enjoyed the problem of cleansing the corrupt mess he had found. He enjoyed the applause of his friends. Lodge wrote from Washington to express his admiration: 'I don't wonder you are receiving letters from all over the country, for you are doing brilliantly. You are making a great place and reputation for yourself which will lead surely to even better things.'[29]

Many may still remember the image of Roosevelt, in caricature, on the stage, or in the press, disguised by enormous green goggles and characterized by glaring rows of teeth, breaking his way into saloons to arrest their keepers for violation of the Sunday excise law. This was altogether too strict, in his own opinion; 'but I have no honorable alternative save to enforce it, and I *am* enforcing it to the furious rage of the saloon-keepers and of many good people too.'[30]

He tramped the streets of New York at night to find out by personal inspection how the police were doing their duty. At times he went forty hours at a stretch without any sleep, proud of his own performance and finding great fun in his midnight rambles. Hitherto he had felt that the weakness of civic virtue lay in its academic nature. With the police he was accomplishing reform without any touch of theory. 'My whole work brings me in contact with every class of people in New York as no other work possibly could: and I get a glimpse of the real life of the swarming millions. Finally I do feel that I am accomplishing a good deal.'[31]

He enjoyed fighting. He delighted in representing himself as a protagonist in the battle of reform. In the most important city of America he felt himself to be the most important character. 'I do not believe that any other man in the United States, not even the President, has had as heavy a task as I have had during the past ten months.'[32] Roosevelt was always able to dramatize every situation in which he found himself, and remove it from the drabness which others would alone have seen. He then represented himself breasting a storm of gigantic grandeur and alone confronting the forces of evil. Unaided, he had to contend with the hostility alike of Tammany and of the Republican machine.

He had, in fact, run foul of the latter. His personality was too strong, his character too individual, to remain confined within the mediocrity of an organization whose leadership he disliked and whose vulnerable sides he denounced. He saw in politics something more than the mere machinery of organization and the wish for place, woven around hackneyed formulas. His idea of duty was not one of lip service to an accepted platform, but meant something far more real. He created a new pattern for the politician. Always he filled the posts he occupied to the fullest measure of their expansion and gave to these an individuality which others before him had left undiscovered.

Roosevelt was never averse to allowing the picturesque side of his personality to offer its appeal to the public. His critics have been inclined to fasten on these accidentals in order to reproach him with striving for sensation and seeking the applause of the multitude. If such criticism is not entirely unjustified, it also, unfairly, loses sight of two striking character-

istics. Roosevelt possessed to a remarkable degree
the instinct of play. He loved children and had the
ability to amuse them, a talent which is akin to the
theatrical instinct. Also he delighted in picturesqueness for its own sake. He had always been in revolt
against the dull composure of prosperous life in New
York. His personal sympathy for so many individuals
who were his inferiors in station, in breeding, and in
education was no affectation, nor were these friendships made merely for political reasons. Such motives
may at first have entered into his calculations, but
were far from being the only factor. In his earlier
years he had derived enjoyment in astonishing his
family by the incongruous nature of his acquaintances, and in after life these predilections became a
second nature. He relished his own ability to make
friends in every station of life, and enjoyed, as few
men have ever done, the possession of that feeling
expressed by a great Father of the Church, who
declared that he was a man and that nothing human
was foreign to him. Of no one could this ever be said
more truly than of Roosevelt.

The enormous driving power he put into his work
for reform was, however, unable to maintain any
sustained enthusiasm on the part of the public. A
great city like New York arouses itself spasmodically
and then relapses into indifference. This apathy was
profoundly discouraging to Roosevelt. He had taken
on himself the hatred of all the corrupt forces in the
great city, for which the good citizens whose battles
he had been fighting were not even grateful. In consequence he passed through hours of profound de-

pression, disgusted by 'the greed and the timidity of our men of means.' The early delight aroused by the novelty of his duties had worn off and the old feeling of restlessness which he had felt so often before again swept over him. A brief visit to Lodge in Washington revived the pleasure of life in the capital in contrast to that of New York. He wrote to his sister: 'We are fairly reveling in the congenial surroundings, so much more congenial than New York in its social side.... There is no society in New York which makes up in any way for the circle of friends whom I have found so congenial here.' [33]

The appreciation of his talents by men influential in national politics stood out in striking contrast to his failure to achieve a political position in his native city. A speech of his against Senator Hill drew from Senator Hoar an enthusiastic telegram, that it was the best speech made on the American continent in thirty years. Lodge kept dangling before him the prize of the New York Senatorship, and encouraged him with the eventual hope of the Presidency. 'I do not say that you are to be President to-morrow. I do not say it will be — I am sure that it may and can be. I do say that the Senate, which is better, is well within reach. If you were like most men, I should not repeat these things to you, but you so underrate your political strength that I fear you will neglect to use it and so miss the opportunity which will give you a big place in national politics.' [34] Roosevelt wrote in answer that he had as much chance of being a United States Senator as of being Czar of Russia. His mercurial temperament swayed between elation and

moods of the utmost depression. He felt lonely and
isolated. In New York he was then at war with almost every politician. There was no one in the metropolis to whom he could unburden himself, no one
for whom he really cared.

'I make acquaintances very easily, but there are
only one or two people in the world, outside of my
own family, whom I deem friends or for whom I
really care.'[35]

Roosevelt felt depressed because he had alienated
the regular Republican organization in New York and
the avenues of political preferment in his native city
seemed closed to him. He had been read out of the
party and the outlook was black. He racked his brain
to find some fearful shortcoming on his own side to
account for the fact that he had not one New York
City newspaper or New York City politician of note
to help his fight. The feeling that he was at the end
of his career again obsessed him. Toward the close
of his tenure as Police Commissioner, he remarked to
a friend that this would be the last office he would
ever hold. He had offended so many powerful interests and so many powerful politicians that no political
preferment would in the future be possible.[36]

Lodge wrote to cheer him out of his depression.
The men who seemed so important to Roosevelt in
New York City looked pretty small in the State
and were absolutely unknown outside. His letters
gave Roosevelt comfort and pleasure. His depression
vanished like a passing mood. The Venezuelan
trouble with England stirred him. 'Let the fight come
if it must — we would take Canada.'[37] A few days

ater, he hoped the fight would come soon. 'The
clamor of the peace faction has convinced me that
his country needs a war.' [38]

He was thinking of other things than New York
politics. He kept saying to himself that he was
thankful he had taken the police commissionership,
and that he was rather prouder of this than of any
work he had ever performed, but his heart was no
longer in his work, and his restlessness caused him to
clamor for fresh interests. 'If it wasn't wrong, I
should say that personally I would rather welcome
a foreign war,' he wrote to Mrs. Cowles.[39] He hated
the feeling of possibly impending idleness. 'The only
thing I am afraid of is that by and by I will have
nothing to do... it is very difficult for me not to wish
for a war with Spain.' [40]

His interest had turned to Cuba. He wanted to
interfere, to drive out the Spaniards, and his thoughts
traveled incessantly in that direction. 'Though I
feel very strongly indeed on such questions as municipal reform and civil service reform, I feel even more
strongly on the questions of our attitude towards the
outside world with all that it implies, from seacoast
defense and a first-class navy to a properly vigorous
foreign policy. I think we ought to interfere in
Cuba.' [41] Writing to his brother-in-law, Captain
Cowles, he asks why, on our new battleships, are we
putting in four- and five-inch quick-firers instead of
six-inch and why do we prefer the rapid-fire six-
pounder to the Gatling and the Hotchkiss? His
thoughts were wandering very far from the New York
police.

X

The McKinley Presidential campaign of 1896, with its bitter fight over the gold standard, aroused Roosevelt's enthusiasm, with the feeling that it was the most important election since the Civil War. Long before the campaign became active, he had met Mark Hanna and advised him that the only way to obtain party contributions in Massachusetts was through Lodge and his friends. In turn he counseled Lodge to cultivate the Ohioan as much as he could, and to handle carefully Hanna's imperious and somewhat narrow personality. Later, with Lodge, he made successful speeches in the Middle West. He spoke often and widely in this campaign and felt some self-satisfaction with the part he had taken in the contest.

His own position was somewhat anomalous. In Washington, Roosevelt was already well known, and in the country at large many men admired him and were interested in his career. His reputation as a reformer of courage had grown considerably. But in his native city his unwillingness to be a docile tool of the machine made him hated by the party leaders, who regarded him as eccentric, cantankerous, and sensational. In the National Government he could have filled any place with distinction, but the smallest place was difficult to obtain so long as he lacked the support of the New York organization. Under our political system, inherited from more rudimentary times, such weakness is an almost fatal bar. How many men admirably fitted for high position have been cast aside from preferment because disliked by a few party hacks!

Roosevelt would hardly admit to himself that his interest in the police was over. He rather hoped to be legislated out of office. Soon after the election, Lodge visited McKinley to try to interest him in the appointment of his friend as Assistant Secretary of the Navy. It was not a very exalted post, but, such as it was, even this he found difficult to obtain. McKinley was complimentary — later Roosevelt called him 'a regular jollier' — but he remained evasive and expressed concern about Roosevelt having some preconceived plan which he might wish to put through as soon as he got in. Lodge assured him of the contrary and pressed for it as a personal favor. The difficulty was with Platt and how the New York organization would relish the appointment of a man so disliked. Lodge talked it over with Platt himself, and the latter, although expressing personal regard, feared lest Roosevelt should utilize his position in order to control the petty patronage of the Brooklyn Navy Yard in a manner hostile to him. In the end, Platt professed to be persuaded and promised to write to the President-elect to urge the appointment. But still it hung fire.

Roosevelt, who had waited expectantly, began to feel depressed about his prospects. A terrible waste of time and strain are suffered in American political life by nearly every one who aspires, successfully or otherwise, to office. The concentration of the power of appointment in the hands of the President, the devious motives which lead to his exercise of this right invite a pressure on the Chief Executive which clogs the roads to preferment and forces those who expect

Government posts, to wait, often in gnawing idleness, until their fate has been decided in accordance with the real or supposed dictates of political expediency.

Roosevelt felt that not having the necessary political backing in his own State and suffering from the hatred of the machine leaders, the odds were against his appointment. For months he was kept on tenterhooks. The position in the Navy Department appealed to him, but he was afraid to allow his hopes to be vainly aroused. He repeated to his relatives that it was not a big place and to Lodge that he did not want to appear as a supplicant. It hurt his pride to ask, as it has galled the pride of many a man in American political life to beg for office. He had already made up his mind that if he should not be appointed, he would continue in the Police Department of New York City so long as he could and then turn to any work offered.

Lodge brought up his reënforcements to press for Roosevelt. Wolcott asked the President as a personal favor; Long, the Secretary of the Navy, was sympathetic. Later, Hay and Taft both spoke warmly in his behalf, as did the Vice-President. Even Hanna proved friendly; but still nothing happened. Just as Roosevelt had abandoned hope, word came that the New York local organization had advised Platt to favor him as Assistant Secretary. His own belief that the machine wished to see him in the post in order to get him out of the city was probably correct. When early in April, after a four-months' campaign, the appointment was made, with Speaker Reed's assistance, Roosevelt telegraphed Lodge that 'Sinbad has evidently landed the old-man-of-the-sea.'

Soon he was again in Washington among friends. He could turn his back on New York, forget his fights with the politicians, and no longer wax indignant at the indifference to good government of the prosperous citizens. The local side of his interests was half forgotten. He felt glad he was out of the mess he had been in. He hated the New York organization, but a relic of party loyalty or prudence had kept him from openly attacking it. In the fall campaign he wrote to Lodge, after he had taken the stump, away from his native city: 'The really ugly feature in the Republican canvass [in New York] is that it *does* represent exactly what the Populists say, that is, corrupt wealth... the Pierpont Morgan type of men forced Fitch on the ticket; and both Platt and Tracy represent the powerful, unscrupulous politicians who charge heavily for doing the work — sometimes good, sometimes bad — of the bankers, railroad men, insurance men, and the like.' [42]

He was no longer in New York politics. His heart and work were in the Navy and its new duties appealed to him immensely. Although he never showed any personal inclination to become a sailor, the naval profession represented what was closest to his taste, the human element in its most manly expression, disciplined in the service of the State. This was another aspect of the same task he had handled in the police force. But how different was the atmosphere! Instead of the intrigues of politicians and the background of corruption, his problem was now to

overcome the inertia of a spineless bureaucracy amid
the indifference of the Administration. He took pride
in the service and made friends and allies with officers
like Evans and Taylor, Sampson and Wainwright, who
seconded admirably the work of preparing the fleet
for the task before it.

Instead of midnight walks of inspection in the
streets of New York, he now visited navy yards and
warships. When a torpedo boat met with an accident,
his official report stated that it was more important
for such vessels to be handled with dash than to be
kept unscratched. If a naval officer had to err, let him
do so on the side of too much daring rather than too
much caution. He spoke before the Naval War College at Newport on the subject of national preparedness. His address reiterated opinions which he had
proclaimed before and which he was often to expound
again, but which now for the first time began to attract national attention.

The frequent repetition of the ideas advanced in
this lecture has caused critics who have approached
Roosevelt's personality from a narrow point of view
to be captious over the obviousness of his statements
and the emphatic redundant commonplaces of his
language. Roosevelt would have been the first to
admit this. There are chapters in his prose, notably
in the experiences of his childhood, which show that
on occasion he could be a master of the craft of words.
But in his public utterances his purpose was never to
gain the applause of the few, but to place his ideas in
their most rudimentary form before the people. Once,
in a lecture before Harvard undergraduates, he dwelt

on how Greek civilization, with all its refinements, had been defeated by the coarser grain of the Romans, and ended his talk with the characteristic words, 'I'm damned glad they did it.'

The lessons he preached were always the same, for his opinions underwent as little evolution as his character. Deliberately he reduced all ideas to their simplest expression, knowing that anything new takes time to filter through the unreceptive mass. At first he found a refractory or apathetic medium for his opinions. It was only by hammering over and over again on the same anvil that he forged his weapons. The fact that his ideas became so generally accepted as to make them commonplace is perhaps the greatest tribute to his success in influencing the American people toward assuming duties which must go with high ambition.

Roosevelt's earliest interest as an historian had led him to write the 'History of the Naval War of 1812.' Afterward he had been greatly impressed with the doctrines of Captain Mahan and the importance of sea power as an instrument of executive policy. Long before the country had even dimly begun to apprehend its later destiny, Roosevelt had dreamed of this. Now he was to have the opportunity of preparing the Navy for the crisis in Cuba.

For years the revolution in that island had been arousing our feelings of sympathy with the Cuban rebels and of indignation against the Spaniards. The horrors incident to the insurrection, the misery visited on hundreds of thousands of innocent people, and especially the inability of Spain either to suppress

the revolt or to restore order, created an atmosphere
eventually favorable to our intervention. Cleveland
had resisted this pressure, just as McKinley had done
during the early part of his Administration when he
earned from Roosevelt the epithet of possessing the
backbone of a chocolate éclair. To Roosevelt anything seemed better than the continuance of Spanish
rule. Before he had ever looked forward to becoming
the Assistant Secretary of the Navy, he hoped that
we would drive the Spaniards out of Cuba.[43]   The
island seemed to him, in fact, an American Crete,
which at that time was suffering under Turkish rule,
and England's action in blockading the Greek insurgents was no less disgraceful in his opinion than
our conduct in not expelling the Spaniards from
Cuba.[44]

At last he was to have a hand in preparing the
Navy for the impending crisis. In September, 1897,
more than six months before war broke out, he submitted a plan to President McKinley for the disposition of the fleet. Its most remarkable feature was his
foresight with regard to the Philippines. At a time
when no other American had even dimly realized the
possibility of our ever becoming interested in a group
of islands which seemed little more than a geographi-
cal expression, Roosevelt was already planning to
have our navy blockade and if possible take Manila.[45]
To his credit must be put the happy choice of Admiral Dewey to command the Asiatic Squadron and
the steps he took to have the ships ready to sail for the
Philippines without delay and destroy the Spanish
fleet in Manila Bay. No one else had foreseen this

likelihood and Dewey himself was at first reluctant to go, fearing that he would find nothing to do beyond playing golf at Hongkong. To Roosevelt's initiative and careful preparation more than to the efforts of any other man we owe the acquisition of the Philippines and the entrance of America as a world power.

XI

The Spanish War was the first great event in Roosevelt's life. His career hitherto had been honorable, interesting, and even distinguished, but it lacked something to raise it from its spasmodic and half-amateurish character. He had dabbled with varying success in many occupations. His talents had been appreciated, his courage and energy admired. But his star had hitherto followed a somewhat eccentric course and it was difficult to discern whether it was on the ascendant or the decline. If Roosevelt had died before Santiago, the eulogist could hardly have gone beyond the vague promise his career had held out.

The events of a few days, in which he played a very gallant but not very important part, suddenly raised him to enduring fame, gave him nation-wide popularity, and placed him on the highroad to the greatest political success. A wild charge which began in the jungle ended in the White House. A brief command, a brief fight, a brief war, as insignificant in its military aspects as it was significant in its political results, made the colonel of a volunteer regiment the most important man in the United States and ended by making him the greatest world figure of his time.

Public opinion, groomed and primed, with a pent-up enthusiasm waiting to acclaim a hero, in this instance at least discerned the right man.

Roosevelt was never prouder of anything in his life than of his charge up San Juan Hill. Afterward, when he expressed regret that his children would have to divide a small inheritance, he felt that along with his sword he had left them a name of which they could be proud and which in some degree would be a substitute for money. His conduct on that hot summer day was deserving of the highest praise, and the author of 'Hero Tales in American History' himself added a chapter to the story. Abundant testimony by officers of the Regular Army shows the magnificent courage he displayed in leading his regiment on horseback across the open ground against a strongly entrenched enemy. Nor was his performance merely one of foolhardy valor. He maintained that it was not reckless, for if he wanted to get the best out of his men, he felt it incumbent to assume all the risks which he asked them to take.

The exploit of Santiago was far from being the chance occurrence of a lucky day. The artist's instinct in Roosevelt half acquiesced in a legend which raised him to quick renown as the improvised leader of Western cowpunchers and Eastern clubmen, and slurred over the careful preparation of many years on his part, in thought, in word, and in act, which rightly made him the residuary legatee of the Spanish War. The different men he had known out West and in the East in the course of his varied experiences — policemen and college men, reformers and politicians,

ROOSEVELT AS A ROUGH RIDER

bankers and cowboys, men who lived among books
and men who never opened a book — separated by
everything else, yet found a common link in their
admiration for Roosevelt. The seeds he had sown
profusely all his life suddenly ripened for him to
garner their harvest.

Years before, when living on his Dakota ranch and
the prospect of trouble with Mexico loomed up,
Roosevelt had hoped for war and intended to raise
some companies of horse riflemen among 'the harum-
scarum rough-riders.' Time and again he had
brooded over the thought of war with the intention
of taking part. When difficulties with England
threatened over Venezuela, his hopes were aroused.
The Cuban crisis gave him new zest, and six months
before hostilities broke out, he told President McKinley that he would go to the war. When the President
asked him what Mrs. Roosevelt would think of this,
he replied that while she would regret his decision,
he would not consult her.

Three weeks later he wrote Lodge [46] that he had
'finally developed a playmate who fairly walked me
off my legs; a Massachusetts man, moreover, an
army surgeon named Wood.' Out of this friendship,
the Rough-Rider idea developed, and it is to the
credit of Roosevelt's real generosity that he suggested Wood for the command of the regiment which
from the first he could have obtained for himself.
The story of the Rough-Riders is so well known that
no useful purpose can be served in repeating time-
worn facts. It would withal be an error to think of
Roosevelt's participation in the campaign only from

the point of view of a patriotic and picturesque gallant adventure. His mind ran seemingly along a single channel, but many different thoughts contributed to his decision to fight and no entreaties of his closest friends and relatives could stop him.

In an extremely interesting letter that Roosevelt wrote to Dr. Sturgis Bigelow, of Boston, on the eve of the Spanish War, he gives the reasons which made him wish to enlist: 'I like life very much. I have always led a joyous life. I like thought and I like action and it will be very bitter to me to leave my wife and children; and while I think I could face death with dignity I have no desire before my time has come to go out into the everlasting darkness.' [47]

No Roman stoic could have written more fittingly than Roosevelt, the churchgoer, who spoke of death not as the life to come but as 'an everlasting darkness.' Having preached what were known as 'Jingo doctrines,' he felt that his power of usefulness would be gone if he did not live up to the ideals he had tried to expound. In a statement of his conduct, his first thought was not of duty, nor adventure, but the wish to justify the lessons he had preached. The Spanish War in this respect was a convenient incident which made it 'important from the standpoint of the Nation as a whole that men like myself should go to war.'

All this was the truth, but was it the only reason? It was not the Assistant Secretary of the Navy who left his office to fight. It was Theodore Roosevelt, who in his career as a citizen advocating national preparedness had incidentally occupied various official positions. It was Theodore Roosevelt, whom every motive now pushed forward to accept the risk of battle. All his tastes, his experiences, and his ambition, whether as a sportsman and a hunter, a ranchman, a reformer, an historian, a citizen, and a politician — all urged him into the fray even against the advice of his closest friends. He would have been untrue to himself had he acted otherwise. In this sense there is a unity in his varied career which made the preparation of a lifetime culminate in one heroic deed.

Others in the army displayed equal courage in the fight at Santiago — Roosevelt himself, with the instincts of a military leader, lavished praise on his men for their gallantry. But there was no one else in the entire army who was then in a position to benefit politically by his deeds. No other man had prepared the soil in the same careful way. The lightning of politics flashes in our heavens with less waywardness than many suppose, and fame earned by martial deeds does not often lead to the highest political preferment. Dewey, for instance, returned with the far greater laurels of Manila Bay, only to become pitiable by the naïve Presidential ambition suggested to him.

Roosevelt's previous political experiences now served him admirably. His exploit had won for him inordinate and widespread popularity. His leadership and his gallantry had alike made an enormous impression on the country. In his private letters to friends and relatives he exulted at the part he had played. His first fear that he would only be a 'fake hero' and not see any fighting soon passed away. After Santiago, when he felt sure of his ground, he proudly contrasted the efficient way in which he had handled his regiment with the confusion and incompetence elsewhere. He wrote to Lodge that there had never been so criminally incompetent a general as Shafter, and not since the expedition against Walcheren had there been grosser mismanagement.[48] Private opinions to intimates expressed pride that he should have been able to lead and handle his men as no one else could. Public utterances and later writings about his regiment and the Cuban campaign were admirable in their temper and taste.

The generosity of his praise for his subordinates won him more friends. When he recommended five men to be promoted for bravery, incidentally he mentioned the fact that two of these were Protestants, two Catholics, and one was a Jew, but their creed he declared was a pure coincidence. After Santiago had fallen, he gave publicity to the famous round robin asking for the transfer of the army to the United States to escape disease. This brought on his head the wrath of the War Department, but won the thanks of the troops. His enemies tried vainly to discredit him for his lack of discipline and to injure his prospects by bringing out the poor opinion he had expressed of a New York National Guard regiment which, armed with obsolete rifles, had behaved none too well. The tide was rising so rapidly in his favor that nothing seemed to injure him.

The fight was hardly over before the newspapers

had nominated Roosevelt for Governor of New York. Lodge wrote from the Senate that he heard continual talk about his being run for Governor or Congressman, and that he could obtain almost anything he wanted. His own desires for Roosevelt went toward the Senatorship and he suggested that he could probably be elected to the House during his absence in the army and come back into public life with an immense enthusiasm behind him. Later, the seat in Congress would surely lead to the Senate.

Roosevelt, then still in camp near Santiago, while elated was also a little dazed. Nation-wide fame had come to him of a sudden, and the wish for office was only part of his ambition for achievement. Though he were to die to-morrow, he felt now he could at least leave his children a name in which they would find pride, and perhaps also the coveted medal of honor which the War Department remained unwilling to give him, for his conduct in spite of its gallantry was professionally not regarded as having gone beyond the normal call of duty. As for politics, he was enough of a soldier to wish to keep in command of his regiment while there was still fighting to do, enough of a politician not to pronounce himself before the time, and enough of a philosopher to appreciate the fickleness of popularity.

'The good people in New York at present seem to be crazy over me; it is not very long since on the whole they felt I compared unfavorably with Caligula. By the time election day comes round, they may have reverted to their former feeling,' he wrote to Lodge.[49] He felt misgivings over his ability to get on in politics, particularly with the New York politicians, and dreaded lest the favor of the multitude should last only a few days. When all had been said, he longed ardently for national politics instead of police boards, and wanted to have the opportunity to handle real questions and not merely petty patronage.

Roosevelt began by taking calmly the movement to nominate him for Governor. His recollections as Police Commissioner still rankled. If popular feeling for him was strong enough, he thought that he would be nominated and elected, but if it was only temporary, he would be neither. For once he felt that no effort of his own could affect the outcome in any way. If it came, well and good; if not, he intended to take the result with philosophy and 'a certain sense of relief' and would then turn again to literary work. He wanted time to digest this recent experience. The fame which came from his conduct as a soldier had given him a satisfaction which, perhaps, he feared to lose if hazarded again in politics.

The Republican organization in New York knew that the political situation made Roosevelt the only candidate with whom they could hope to win. The nomination was offered him after a preliminary inquiry as to whether he would 'make war' on Platt and his friends. His answer that he did not want to make war on any one, and that he wished to be Governor of the State and not a faction leader, clinched the matter for a nomination which was never a choice but a necessity.

XII

No one who resides in the Executive Mansion at Albany can fail to remember that Martin Van Buren and Grover Cleveland, before they became Presidents, had both been Governors of New York. There are two great roads to political preferment in the United States, and Van Buren and Cleveland in different ways have each been typical of these. The first reached the White House after long and faithful service rendered in behalf of the Democratic organization of his State, and the latter arrived by a few short cuts which impressed themselves on the popular imagination. Roosevelt's position in the party resembled more that of Cleveland. He had come to the front by the strength of his own personality. He was distrusted by the leaders. He lacked the patience and the temperament to adjust his step to the discipline of the machine, and he could neither capture that organization nor build up one of his own.

His public methods were very different from those of Cleveland or from any hitherto known in our political life. He often spoke of himself as a practical idealist, or a reformer in politics. His ideas had been learned from reformers, his practices from politicians, and neither could forgive him for taking half their doctrine and rejecting the rest. But the artist's sense of picturesqueness was all his own. The tactics he followed were in part deliberate intention, in part the workings of natural instincts. Roosevelt knew that he would never have made a success of pure organization politics. His originality was too great not to strike out an individual line.

Long experience also had taught him how rootless was the ground of pure reform. He despised the anæmic nature of its academic background. Deliberately he planted his personal pennant in the midst of that vast electorate who are called the people and on whom in final analysis party organization, or reform, is obliged to count. His ambition had always been to lead the people. The success of his career depended on his ability to accomplish this, for without the popular support he received the politicians would have made short shrift of him. His magnificent vitality and the warmth of his personality were indispensable in order to rouse a normally lethargic mass to a level of enthusiasm which carried him forward as its leader, irrespective of the party organization. From the time he became Governor to his dying day, the successes and failures of his public career depended on his ability to maintain this contact.

Many politicians have tried this. The popular appeal, more especially with the Democratic Party, is the open road along which every ambitious man desires to travel. In our own day both Bryan and Wilson have essayed it with varying success. Its difficulty lies in sustaining sufficient support for a leader beyond the artificial fever of the elections. Roosevelt's achievement lay in prolonging this. He never allowed interest in himself or in his measures to flag. The ordinary politician, safely returned to power, lapses into a routine programme whittled down to dimensions acceptable to his organization. Not so Roosevelt, who, whether in public or in pri-

vate life, was always the best company in the world.
His technique was as obvious as it has remained
inimitable.

The Governorship of New York provided his first
great opportunity. He knew that he had reached the
office by an accident and that the Spanish block-
houses of Santiago were easier to storm than the
Platt machine in New York. He understood that the
post might either be his last chance or else the beginning of a great career. In American political life
few men think of the office they hold except in terms
of the next. Roosevelt did that and more. He enjoyed the Governorship thoroughly, just as he enjoyed every opportunity for action, but he was under
no illusions as to the permanence of his position. It
included what might be called a sporting chance for
higher things. Six months before he was nominated
for Vice-President, he wrote to Lodge, 'If McKinley
were to die to-morrow, I would be one of the men
seriously *considered* as his successor — I mean that
and just no more.' [50]

Many 'ifs' are planted along the road to the White
House and Roosevelt's ambition soared too high to
be confined to any office for its own sake. Albany was
a convenient platform and a stepping-stone. So long
as he was Governor, he would remain in the popular
eye in an interesting manner and justify his own
meteoric rise.

Under the surface, ran other dangerous currents.
Roosevelt might be Governor, but the power and the
funds of the Republican organization remained in
Senator Platt's hands. For Platt, Roosevelt had been

an intruder, a sensation-mongering political adventurer, unsafe in his methods, forced upon him by circumstances over which he had no control, and whom he had been obliged to use as a temporary expedient. Roosevelt has not ordinarily been associated in the public estimate with diplomatic skill, although later in the White House he displayed talents of the highest order. As Governor, his relations with Platt provided occasion for the exercise of very real diplomacy. From the start he had to measure his strength and compare it with the solid disciplined phalanx at the Senator's disposal. He lacked support. Roosevelt knew he could place himself occasionally at the head of public opinion when he had roused sufficient enthusiasm behind him. But methods of this kind had to be sparingly utilized or they would go stale. He understood that he had neither the training nor the capacity to match Platt and his machine and in the end the advantage must lie on the side of the professionals. Roosevelt's purpose wisely was to avoid useless fighting and steer the middle course. He felt no inherent dislike for Platt; he rarely had an inherent dislike for any man. His distaste was for certain types of men, and if occasionally he pilloried an individual it was intentionally in order to single him out as incarnating some noxious idea. The politician in him appreciated the necessity for a disciplined organization and envied Platt for possessing this. In fact the only breaches in discipline which Roosevelt ever condoned were those he himself committed.

He was never submissive to Platt. This would

THE CHAMPION ROUGH RIDER OF THE WORLD

have been repugnant to his native masterfulness and
politically a mistake. In his 'Autobiography' he
states that it was necessary to have it understood at
the outset that 'the Administration was my Administration and was no one else's but mine.' [51]
A minor part as Governor would have detracted
from his reputation for independence, lessened his
personality, and weakened the confidence reposed by
supporters who admired in him the reformer. Skill-
fully he traced his path between these two extremes
with seeming indifference and real care.

Both Platt and Roosevelt were anxious to avoid
open warfare detrimental to every one. Almost the
only great losing fight the Senator made was over
Lou Payn, the Superintendent of Insurance, whom
the Governor, for excellent reasons, refused to re-
appoint, at the same time stating that he was ready
to accept another organization man. Roosevelt has
narrated this incident with considerable gusto. He
relished its humor, enjoyed his personal victory, and
rejoiced in being able to resist the threats made at
Platt's suggestion that the refusal would ruin his
career. Roosevelt was too independent to be deterred
by menace, and too good a politician to be intimidated
by bluff, particularly when he knew he was right. He
suggests that his refusal was based on moral courage.
It was as much due to political acumen.

Roosevelt's wisdom as Governor came in singling
out a few measures in which he appeared conspicu-
ously before the public and fighting in its interest,
although to do so he had to cut loose from the machine. Most notable was his victory in obtaining the

taxation of public franchises, which, it was then
feared, would dry up a great corrupt source of party
funds. Platt sincerely believed that this measure
was akin to the most dangerous expressions of Western populism. With greater discernment Roosevelt
forced through this bill. The elemental justice of his
contention appears more manifest to-day than it
did at that time. The self-evident desirability of the
measures he advocated tends to obscure the fact that
he was the first public man to apply these. His supreme merit was not the novelty of progressive ideas
which he borrowed freely from others, but lay in the
fact that in adopting these he was sufficiently in
touch with the great body of the electorate to remain persuasive. If the American people can feel
that many of the innovations of yesterday have
become the commonplaces of to-day, high credit is
due to Roosevelt.

To his sister he wrote at the end of his term:
'Seriously, I think I can say with absolute truthfulness that I have administered this Governorship
better than it has ever been administered before in
my time.'[52] Nor was this vanity on his part. He
had said much the same thing before, as Civil Service
Commissioner, as Police Commissioner, and as Colonel of the Rough Riders. It was the not over-modest
self-analysis of a man whose exuberance forced him
to express himself to his intimates, sometimes in
praise, at other times in detraction.

As Governor, Roosevelt had enhanced his reputation, put through some excellent legislation, asserted
sufficient independence in a conspicuous manner, and

yet not quarreled too outrageously with the machine. There was no love lost between him and Platt, but also there had been no open breach. Platt henceforth had to reckon with him. He was a force in New York politics and had already developed into a national figure of great prominence. Lodge kept telling him that he was a Presidential possibility of the future. His ambitions were shaped for the White House. Meanwhile, the two alternatives before him were the Vice-Presidency or another term at Albany.

XIII

The Vice-Presidency was the only office Roosevelt ever occupied in which he did not and could not distinguish himself. It was the only office he ever held which he had tried his utmost to avoid. His position was understandable. In the summer of 1899 he had been out West to attend his regimental reunion at Las Vegas. At every station at which the train stopped, from Indiana to New Mexico, he was received by crowds as if he had been a Presidential candidate. To avoid offense at the White House, he gave out an interview stating that he favored McKinley's renomination and also Vice-President Hobart's if the latter would accept. Yet, when the Vice-Presidency had first been suggested, Roosevelt listened sympathetically. He knew that his hold in New York was precarious, and he was then looking around for any suitable position that offered. He would have far preferred to be Secretary of War, or best of all a United States Senator, but of that he saw no possibility. The chance of being President seemed slim. In another four years' time the recollection of the Spanish War would be remote and his record as Governor no longer recent. He desired most of all to become Governor-General of the Philippines, or a Cabinet officer, perhaps eventually even a Senator. If he accepted the Vice-Presidency, he would remain 'planted' for four years in a wearisome place.

Lodge, from his angle as Senator, was not convinced by this argument, though he felt that when a man was candidate for the Presidency no friend had the right to urge him to follow a course against his own judgment.[53] Platt, who oddly professed sympathy with Roosevelt's Presidential aspirations, for this reason was at first opposed to his accepting the Vice-Presidency. Roosevelt, thinking it over, also became more reluctant. He felt that he would be shelved and could do nothing in that position without attracting the President's suspicions and antagonism. Congressman Littauer, who had known him since Harvard, and whom at that time he had publicly called his closest personal friend and political adviser, went to see him about the nomination to confirm these views by relating that the Western Congressmen who admired him were all against his acceptance. He wrote to his sister Mrs. Cowles, in February, 1900, that he had definitely decided not to take the Vice-Presidency and she was at liberty to mention this to any one.

Ambitions of several kinds were then buzzing through his head. Primarily, he wanted to be President in 1904, but as no such hope could be avowed, he had to trim his sails to steer a less hazardous course.

A second term in Albany seemed his best choice and easiest to obtain. He could afterward resign to accept the Governorship of the Philippines.

There were other reasons why he did not want the Vice-Presidency. The money question was serious for him. His means were moderate, his children growing up. As Governor, he was comparatively well paid and enjoyed a residence. But the Vice-Presidency on a salary of $8000 a year would be a serious drain on his resources and would leave him a 'poor man at a frolic.' If there had been real opportunity for something to do, he would not have minded this so much. But to be a figurehead, occupying the only wearisome seat in the Senate, and unable to reply to certain of the Senators whom he most despised, would be too much for his patience. He would find himself in 'a cold shiver of rage' when he could not answer 'the hounds.'

Meanwhile, Platt, whose sympathy had at first been lukewarm, now wanted him for Vice-President, after having promised his support to Odell, although Woodruff was the New York candidate. In Roosevelt's opinion this was due to the pressure of the big moneyed interests on whom the Senator relied for his campaign contributions. These were desirous to get him out of the State, and wished to kick him upstairs in a safe way, for any open attempt to prevent his being renominated would cost too many votes. At the Convention, Roosevelt headed the New York delegation, conspicuous under his Western cowboy hat, and vigorously asserting his wish to remain Governor. Opposing currents, oddly enough, caused his nomination. Platt, who at first feared that he could not prevent Roosevelt's renomination as Governor, started the movement through Quay of Pennsylvania to make Roosevelt Vice-President, and found it taken up with irrepressible enthusiasm by his Western admirers. Conventions develop tempers of their own and the most deliberately made plans have to be thrown over in a moment. In this instance Lodge, seeking the Vice-Presidency for Roosevelt as a road to the White House, and Platt, seeking it to get rid of him in New York State, were alike gratified. Even Hanna, who at first did not want Roosevelt on the ticket because he thought him erratic and un-balanced, yielded to McKinley's wish, who, though he did not welcome him as a running mate, desired to shelve him by making him the presiding officer of the Senate.

The nomination came to Roosevelt while he sat in a hotel bedroom at Philadelphia reading 'Josephus,' as his sister notes. He was soon reconciled. The enormous enthusiasm of his reception was agreeable, and he wrote to Mrs. Cowles that he would be both ungrateful and a fool not to be deeply touched by the way in which the nomination had come about. He threw himself into the campaign with his customary ardor and a vastly enlarged experience. He made five or six hundred speeches and directly addressed from three to four million people. In his tour, which took him into every part of the country, he greatly enhanced the enormous popularity and personal following which he had already acquired and retained to his dying day. By word and act he impressed him-

THE CAMPAIGN OF 1900

'Well, well, Willie; what is it this time?'
'We're playing Republican minstrels, and Teddy wants to be the
two end men and the middleman, too'

self on vast masses of voters. McKinley as President felt obliged to remain at the White House or on his front porch in Canton, and could take but little part. Roosevelt, by force of circumstance, was the central figure of the campaign which his own personality would in any case have made him. The President's negative virtues seemed to fade still more dimly when championed by the candidate for Vice-President. Roosevelt was then at the height of his ability. He had acquired an impressive power of expression in simple, forceful words, and enjoyed the effects of his own personality and the attention he compelled.

After the election he had still two months more to serve at Albany. His duties as Vice-President presiding over the Senate lasted only one week. A few slips in the routine of the office inspired caricatures representing him hard at work studying parliamentary law. Of more importance was the fact that he then proposed seriously again to take up the study of law in order to be admitted to the bar. How far his intention to practice went, how far it was intended to remedy deficiencies he may have discovered in his scrutiny of legislation at Albany, how far he saw in his proposed study at the law school a useful opportunity to continue to strike the public imagination, will always be uncertain. He spoke to friends of his intention later to practice the legal profession. He wrote that he did not expect to go any further in politics and he could hardly anticipate that a man with 'so many and so loudly and not always wisely expressed convictions' should have gone so far.[54] He had often before said much the same thing. All the time his heart was filled with ambition. He had tasted power and popularity and enjoyed its fruits, and he was determined to let no opportunity slip for his advancement. A tour out West in the summer elated him by the feeling aroused in his behalf from Illinois to Colorado. The trip, he declared, had proved a revelation to him. The men who assured him of their support were important National Committeemen and Congressmen. He attributed their expressions of friendship to the genuine desire of the people and the wish of the politicians to strengthen themselves by coming out for him. Even Platt had volunteered the statement that he would support him when the time came. But Roosevelt did not attach much confidence to his professions, and told all the Western politicians that they must be prepared to have New York against him. He felt convinced that his own State would be unfavorable to his claims.[55]

Roosevelt as Vice-President in 1900 was already thinking in terms of the nomination of 1904. No one has ever understood popular psychology so well, and with infinite care he was then preparing the future ground. Speculation is useless in such instances, but the enormous popularity he had acquired allows one to say that, if accident had not made him President before his time, the force of his personality must inevitably have done so at the next election. He did not have to wait. Mr. Dooley's sinister prediction at the Convention that he was bound for the White House, even if his path led through the cemetery, came true at the most unexpected moment. Roosevelt found himself President in the only way which he could not relish.

CHAPTER II

VICTORY

I

'IT shall be my aim to continue absolutely unbroken the policy of President McKinley,' Roosevelt declared when summoned post-haste from a holiday in the Adirondacks to take the oath of office at the murdered President's deathbed. It was no more possible for Roosevelt to become a second McKinley than it would have been for the Ohio politician to copy the Rough-Rider. There had been very little sympathy between the two men, and Roosevelt doubtless felt that the panegyric contained in this first message and his invitation to the members of the old Cabinet to continue in office discharged all obligations to his memory and to the country. Certain Cabinet officers like Hay and Root were already his close advisers and friends, and Knox was soon to become one. Thus there was continuity without similarity in the White House, for Roosevelt had every intention that the Administration should in the fullest sense be his own. 'It is a dreadful thing to come into the Presidency this way; but it would be a far worse thing to be morbid about it,' he wrote to Lodge. The White House had been his natural ambition for years, even when it appeared a dim and distant dream. An anarchist's crime had merely hastened the march of destiny.

The White House, like the greater part of the city

of Washington, is built upon a flat expanse. But its
principal occupant is suddenly raised to heights
known to no other mortal, in which he breathes an
air very different from that of ordinary humanity.
The sense of power provides the greatest of intoxi-
cants, for even after power has vanished, its effect
never wears off. To his last day Roosevelt preserved
undimmed the memory of the authority he was to
wield during seven years, and the ardent wish to regain this never ceased to haunt him. The Presidency
for Roosevelt was the only time in his life when his
dominant wish for power and the ability to gratify
its exercise swayed in balance. At last he could put
into practice ideas which he had nurtured since
youth. A character so firmly set, strongly marked,
and early matured, needed the opportunity of the
highest office which uncovers the weak and girds the
strong.

The first message which as President he addressed
to Congress gave little ground for controversy. It
recommended that 'some at least of the forest reserves should afford perpetual protection to the
native fauna and flora, safe havens of refuge to our
rapidly diminishing wild animals of the larger kind,
and free camping-grounds for the ever-increasing
numbers of men and women who have learned to find
rest, health, and recreation in the splendid forests and
flower-clad meadows of our mountains.'

Roosevelt the naturalist and the sportsman now
found occasion to stimulate interest in nature and
promote a taste which he had always possessed, and
which was intended to lead to a more solicitous care

for the beauty of our wilds. The feudal Old-World tradition of personal ownership of vast estates is foreign to our soil. The President endeavored to obtain the equivalent through creating great national domains which, by their promise of health-giving pastime for all, might fit into the frame of American life. There was nothing new in these ideas. Roosevelt had cherished the lure of the wilderness since boyhood and all who in America felt delight in free nature shared similar opinions whether able or not to make their expression articulate. Yet rightly they seemed intensely novel to the American people. Originality in a statesman is rarely the discovery of an idea, but the power to secure its application. The public man has to persuade the vast and indifferent aggregates who compose a modern democracy to adopt the opinions of a few till they believe these to be the expression of their own wishes. Who in America first thought of the preservation of natural resources is of as little consequence as is the borrowed origin of Shakespeare's plots to the genius of his poetry. Roosevelt's enthusiasm sprang from his own delight for nature in all its forms. His merit lay in possessing the ability to communicate this to the American people and awaken the desire of a nation to safeguard for unborn generations the beauty of the wilderness as a great popular heritage.

Roosevelt then taught the world that leadership in a republic can be as picturesque as in a monarchy and that a President by his personality can also enrich the life of a people. His interests extended in the most varied directions. He found time to beautify Washington and girdle it with verdure, and lay out parks and drives to adorn the national capital. The task of administration no longer restricted only to drab departmental activity, now ran like a torrent which overflowed in unexpected directions. He called on Stanford White to plan Government buildings of dignity and asked the sculptor Saint-Gaudens to design a new gold currency which brought beauty to our coin. Under him the Presidency came to mean infinitely more than a mere executive. Roosevelt's tastes were so pervasive, he was so many sided, that his office reflected like a mirror his overwhelming activities. John Morley aptly described the President and Niagara Falls as the two most interesting natural phenomena in America.

Foreigners saw mainly forceful energy in Roosevelt. His deepest appeal, which endeared him to the mass of the country, came from the impression he made as a moralist. Deliberately, his action would be attached to some indisputable proposition advanced with a view to bringing out its ethical points. Whenever possible it would be covered by a fundamental American ideal, presented in a striking form, with elemental simplicity intended to convey a meaning easily understood and certain to meet with general approval. The impression he tried to create was one of forceful and impartial righteousness. Partisanship sees only a single side of a question; philosophical skepticism views it with indifference under many aspects. Roosevelt followed his own line between these extremes, usually confining his analysis to clashing alternatives, which with skilled news sense he conveyed to the public in a manner always to justify the course he had adopted.

Secure in the knowledge of how to obtain popular approval, Roosevelt allowed himself greater latitude than any of his predecessors. He knew that millions of 'plain people,' whose confidence he had won and who felt that he had their interest at heart, stood behind him. Farmers, mechanics, and small trades-men learned to regard him peculiarly as their President. This trust made him unwilling to do anything to shatter their belief. On one occasion he related how three old back-country farmers called at the White House. They hadn't a black coat among them and two of them wore no neckties, but they came to say that they believed in him, and one of them told him, 'We want to shake that honest hand.' Roosevelt, touched to the quick by this incident, mentions it among the reasons why he did not seek a third term.

A noticeable influence exercised by the Presidential office on Roosevelt may be observed in the later frequency of his self-designation as a democrat. In common with other statesmen who have not escaped the charge of autocracy, he took pride in asserting the genuine quality of his own democracy, especially after he had been President. The White House pro-vided him with opportunities for reaching the people of the United States which he could have obtained in no other way. Politicians of lesser breed elevated to the highest dignity are more inclined to rest their power on the office, or with the inner control of a party organization, but Roosevelt relied for his on the moral support he received from the masses which was added to his own vast popularity. When later he became a guest of royalty, he was jestingly to express his esteem for the German Emperor by telling him that in America the Kaiser could carry his own election ward. There was a touch of condescension in this compliment, for Roosevelt then felt in himself the ability to carry the entire country.

The instinct for power was intense in his character. The natural sense of leadership within him and the wish for mastery had been gratified by the approval of millions of plain people. No wonder that democracy appealed to him, as it does to any strong man able to inspire, to shape, and to lead a great nation. His enthusiasm might have been less great had he always been relegated to obscurity. But American democracy, as soon as he rose to eminence, provided a medium for the exercise of his highest talents which would have remained stunted under any other system.

Although Roosevelt's good taste left him silent over his future fame, from the time he had reached the Presidency this became a matter of deep concern to him. Alone of his generation in America he possessed the all-around attainments, the boisterous expression, the love of adventure, and the varied talents of the great men of the sixteenth century. Like these he felt no interest in money-making, but a real craving for immortality. Like these he knew his Plutarch, and the heroes of antiquity lived vividly in his mind. Writing from Cuba he had compared Shafter to Crassus in his campaign against the Parthians. His 'Autobiography' and his 'Life' by J. B. Bishop, which he himself had supervised, were prepared

argely with a view to posterity. No untrue word was
ever written in these, but much admittedly is left
unsaid about his political life to raise higher the
pedestal on which he stood. The care he took to write
private letters, particularly when President, even to
men who personally were not close to him, in order to
explain certain actions or describe certain incidents,
and the friends among whom copies of these letters
were circulated, point to a deep-rooted desire to preserve for the future the record of his achievement in
the manner in which he wished it to be known.

He took occasion to leave for posterity even his
theory of the State and justify against criticism the
methods he had employed and which he explains, in
a remarkable letter written to the English historian,
Sir George Trevelyan, a copy of which he gave to the
American historian, J. F. Rhodes. This constitutes
a unique document, for there is probably no other
example of an American President at the end of his
term of office explaining his own political philosophy.

He had used every ounce of power there was in the
Presidential office, without caring a rap for the criticism of those who spoke of his usurpation: 'I believe
that the efficiency of this government depends upon
its possessing a strong central executive, and whenever I could establish a precedent for strength in the
executive, as I did, for instance, as regards external
affairs in the case of sending the fleet around the
world, taking Panama, settling affairs of Santo
Domingo and Cuba... I have felt not merely that my
action was right in itself, but that in showing the
strength of, or in giving strength to, an executive I

was establishing a precedent of value. I believe in
a strong executive; I believe in power; but I believe
that responsibility should go with power and that it is
not well that the strong executive should be a perpetual executive.' [1]

In his judgment there was nothing amiss in the
concentration of power in one man's hands, provided
only that the holder did not keep it for more than a
certain time and then returned it to the people from
whom the power sprang.

II

The dissection of a mind is never easy and any
attempt to analyze the motives of Roosevelt as
President can at best only be fragmentary. Primarily
there entered into his life at the White House a very
lofty idea of the dignity of the Presidential office, an
immense patriotism, an unbounded energy, vitality,
and masterfulness, and a firm ambition to make as
good a President as he knew how. This was strength-
ened by an ardent belief in the righteousness of whatever causes he took up, and in himself as a popular
leader who knew that his hold on the people was
greater than on the party. The further wish to be the
undisputed head of the Republicans was due to a
number of considerations, including an appreciation
of the means necessary to carry out his legislative
measures and later to obtain approval for these at the
polls.

He derived satisfaction as an historian to feel that
he himself was now making history, and as a man of
the world, that he was filling the Presidential office in

the manner in which it ought to be filled. He was
frankly delighted that his position had raised him on
a pedestal to exalt whatever he did. He knew he was
a world figure, the greatest of his time, and in this
knowledge there were modesty and conceit and
shrewd self-estimation all oddly blended. There was
the artist's wish for applause and the gentleman's
wish for effacement, for some of his most important
achievements designedly remained silent. There was
the schoolboy's delight at prowess in company and
the scholar's delight in cultivated conversation.
All these elements in varying proportions were interwoven in his mind and helped to make him the most
picturesque personality who has yet filled the Presidential office.

His Administration appeared to him at the same
time as a solemn duty and an adventure, a game to
play and a lofty mission. During the seven years of
his Presidency it is easy to single out any side of
Roosevelt's colossal activities and interpret this to
the exclusion of other motives. The picture can be
painted in a choice of colors, but never drably. The
new President's character, so forceful, direct, and
seemingly impulsive, was far more complicated and
intricate than is commonly supposed. The ancient
adage about the whole being greater than its parts
was never truer than with Roosevelt.

Those who then watched the intense enjoyment he
felt in all he did knew well that he was no ordinary
mortal. East and West, antiquity and the modern
world, classes and masses, America and Europe, had
contributed to enrich his personality, and he, con-

scious of all he stood for, filled Washington with his
own boisterous delight. Like Leo X, exclaiming that
as God had given him the Papacy he would enjoy it
so Roosevelt also enjoyed to the fullest measure his
Presidential dignity.

In itself the White House provides a natural stage
whose occupants are always of interest to a people
who still preserve an avid curiosity for personal details. With Roosevelt even this setting became almost superfluous. His vitality never flagged in its
picturesque expression. The United States has inherited from its memory of the frontier a deeper
appreciation of physical virtues than other countries.
A fondness for sport in France would, until lately
have covered a politician with ridicule, and in England, although skill as a cricketer may enhance a
public man's popularity, mere muscular strength will
hardly do this. America, even when it smiled at
Roosevelt's athleticism, inwardly felt proud of his
prowess. At the Army and Navy football game
which he attended shortly after he became President
thousands of spectators watched him tearing across
the field, followed with difficulty by the members of
his Cabinet, some of whom, like Long, his former
chief, who was still Secretary of the Navy, panted far
behind him. No more convincing example of the new
President's physical fitness could have been offered to
the public. The people admired while Roosevelt
boxed and wrestled, rode and played tennis. The
famous cross-country hikes which he took with his
intimates began by astonishing Washington and
ended by being accepted as a recognized institution.

Such exploits were not undertaken for effect, but it would be an error to believe that he remained unconscious of the impression they made on the public eye. His own enjoyment of physical deeds had always been keen, and the politician knew how impossible it is for the Chief of State to indulge in any pursuit without attracting attention. When that Chief is both a party and a great popular leader, the example he sets counts for much. Roosevelt in his pastimes gratified his own tastes, but political sense also taught him that he was acting in a manner directly conducive to his popularity. The boyish instincts in his nature made their fond appeal to the inherent and still growing youthfulness of the American people.

Age and youth in a nation are relative expressions and chronologically often topsy-turvy. The Pilgrims, and the Dutch settlers on Manhattan, were far from being either young or primitive in their somber view of life. Even at the end of the eighteenth century, America, conscious of the Old-World ties, was more sophisticated and aged than is the United States of to-day. Youth in a people is induced by physical struggle which leads to visible result and emanates from the free flow of vigor that the spirit takes even when the current below swirls through devious channels. The penalty of the frontier, which exalts the hardier virtues, lies in its depreciation of qualities which are not immediately serviceable. When the frontier fades into an historical memory, the premium on ruder traits ceases until induced again by a taste for adventure which calls for youth. A nation's vision becomes extended once more when new planets swim into its ken.

It was Roosevelt's merit to have given the spark of his own electricity to make America a younger nation, but also one in which the cowboy would not despise the philosopher. He knew that deep down in the people lay a hidden wealth of adventurous idealism which still remained wastefully unshaped, drifting without goal or guidance. McKinley, whose temporizing spirit had moved ill at ease amid unfamiliar events, could never have given to others the feeling of personal leadership which had become necessary at a moment when the aftermath of the Spanish War left world-wide responsibilities confronting the United States. No man in American history could have provided this direction better than Roosevelt, and it was our fortune as a nation that he became President at the very time when he could also be most useful to the country.

His elevation to the Presidency marked the closing of the chapter of crude materialism which followed the Civil War and the inauguration of a new epoch of extended horizon for the United States which coincided in its moral expression with his own character. In later years Roosevelt, in a moment of depression, remarked to a friend that, though he would like to be President again, he knew it was impossible, and he admitted that he was no longer the man needed for the office. His own time and the America he had known best was that of the early years of this century. He understood the country because he himself had done so much to shape its instincts. Then, in the vigor of his manhood, he had personally incarnated the Nation at a moment when it was advancing rapidly in its manifold activities. He had awakened an appreciation of unsuspected values, stirred the imagination of a mighty people and fired it with his own ardor to strive for nobler ends. America, ripe for greatness, had been lacking in realization of purpose, method, and ambition. Roosevelt touched the Nation's pride and made the world bear witness to our merit. Augustus boasted that he found Rome a city built of bricks and left it of marble. So also Roosevelt could proudly say that he had taken America from its hermit state of isolation to lead it along the road of imperial destiny.

III

How far was Roosevelt a politician? Charles S. Washburn, who had known him since Harvard and disagreed with him over many public questions, declared that he never was one. The question hinges on the definition of words. If by politician is implied a man who does things in which he disbelieves, or refrains from doing things which he knows are right only for reasons of likely advancement or popularity, Roosevelt was no politician. He never debased himself in or out of office by recommending measures which he knew in his heart were wrong nor failed to grapple with an issue which he felt lay in his power to solve, merely because it appeared to be dangerous. His career, notably after he had been President, offers the most convincing proof that he did many things which he could not but know from experience to be politically unwise.

Yet no one was ever more adroit or possessed a more minute and practical knowledge of the American people. His industry was enormous and he absorbed facts with sponge-like avidity and held them like a vise. To his extraordinary memory was added wide reading and a fund of general information which impressed politicians who rarely erred on the side of over-education. No detail was too trivial for him not to remember. His mind opened like an index on the most varied subjects and contained a wealth of facts which he submitted usually to sound criteria of judgment.

Many, then, had experience of the minute scrutiny which Roosevelt exercised even in the case of the smallest appointments and the attention he paid to every ounce of political value to be extracted from these. He could tell Senator Bailey of Texas, who was urging him to promote an incompetent army officer on the ground of having the endorsement of his State, that he didn't care a damn for the Legislature of Texas. Yet he was not insensible to recommendations of this kind, as was shown when to avoid criticism he promoted another soldier from the same State. No office was so unimportant that it could be neglected safely, and in considering the applicant's qualifications, those near him were often astonished by his amazingly retentive memory and by the minute information he possessed of local bickerings and even of family quarrels throughout the breadth of the United States. During the New York gubernatorial campaign in 1898, he amazed the Republican organization in his first conference by the detailed knowledge he exhibited of local political conditions in every county of the State.

The party man was strong in Roosevelt, for the remembrance had been branded deep in his mind that until he became President he had suffered from the want of an organization which would effectively support him. He might declare that partisan consideration was secondary to whatever was beneficial to the people, yet he did his utmost to make his own policies identical with the interests of the Republicans. The example of Grover Cleveland, during his second term disrupting the Democratic organization, had not been lost on Roosevelt, who at an early stage decided to use every weapon in his power to keep his party intact as an effective body. He fortified its structure and filled it as rapidly as he could with his own men at the same time that he tried to convert the party to his creed. Republican politics became mingled in his mind with his personal ideas, which reflected the widest nature and most diverse origin.

The real test of the politician, distinguishing him from the layman, does not lie in attributes which popular belief assigns to the former, but in his ability to analyze and quickly weigh the value of currents of opinion. He must be able to decide at once how far opposition to any measure is true, and how far it emanates from hidden or passing causes. He must know when to withstand and when to yield to pressure and appraise the price which invariably has to be paid for legislation or appointment. The ability to discern the real from the spurious and always to be prepared to cast a rapid mental balance calls for a quality of political skill in which Roosevelt was unsurpassed.

Characteristic also of the politician is caution, and Roosevelt was himself far more cautious than is commonly believed. His methods of inquiry before taking a decision were conducted with the utmost prudence. He was artist enough to hide this aspect of his skill, and to serve his dishes without any indication of their ingredients or of the care he had generally taken in their preparation. His method was that of the military commander who conceals his reserves until ready to hurl them at the foe. Roosevelt's system of attack when it came into the open was so frontal that men forgot the wariness of his approach and the craft with which he prepared his onslaught. Humorously it was said of him that, if some one had discovered the mutilated remains of his grandmother in his cellar, he would at once have been able to produce a letter proving his innocence of the crime. No public man has ever conducted so extensive a correspondence or one which has been so little embarrassing to his activities. He felt that it was almost a necessity to record his opinions on everything with a wealth of detail which amazed the reader. One hundred and fifty thousand letters of his are stated to exist. He kept copies of what he wrote, and often, when attacked, his marvelous memory enabled him at once to meet the charge by producing a letter of bygone days which he utilized to confound his adversaries.

Although politics were a means to Roosevelt and never an end, the pleasure derived in the exercise of his craft was due to the artist's knowledge that he was master of its medium. Instinct and long experience had taught him the entire game and made him appreciate the necessity of its workings as a practical means for achievement. Yet there was more than this. The occasional bull rush he exhibited, and the habit of emphatic expression which he cultivated, made men forget that this was only one side of a very varied personality and not the most important. The quality of political evangelist which he often displayed when analyzed contained also a fondness for novelty. There grew in him the wish to interest the American people in whatever he did, and, as occasionally there crept a doubt in his mind of how long this interest would continue, he made a deliberate attempt always to satisfy public appetite with new dishes. From youth his intellectual curiosity had been prone to take pleasure in novelty for its own sake. His distaste for the composure of self-satisfaction which had surrounded his boyhood induced him more easily to erase the surfaces of friction which bar most people from the perception of the new, and made him welcome the latter particularly when it was picturesque. This was more than the expression of a taste. Behind stood the reasoned wish of a public man desirous to lend the prestige of his authority to whatever he thought fitting to advocate to the Nation. Lurking in this complex lay also the satisfaction of personal discovery.

Not all his essays were profitable and even so shrewd a judge of opinion as Roosevelt occasionally erred in his estimate. His endorsement of the new spelling was unfortunate, and his own good taste in seeking to remove from our coinage the motto 'In God we Trust' aroused so unexpected a criticism that he felt it wise to yield. American opinion is often unfairly censorious, and Roosevelt on one occasion found himself blamed for a routine telegram, beginning with the words, 'I and my People,' which had been sent by the State Department in his name to the President of Peru, but which he had never seen.

The impulsive outburst which was supposed to be among his characteristics and even the occasional offense he gave were often intentional. The frequent altercations into which he plunged, the bandying of epithets, and the padded lists of the Ananias Club were not invariably conducive to the dignity of his office. No one was ever more effective in pillorying his adversaries. Inwardly Roosevelt might regret the occasional violence of his language, but if he did so this was in a passing mood and left no chastening mark. The rush of events was too continuous for him to ruminate long over anything.

Almost his first act in the White House, when he invited the Negro educator Booker Washington to dinner, caused an unforeseen stir. Southern opinion stormed indignantly. Characteristically, Roosevelt wrote to express his satisfaction with what he had done: 'I am very glad that I asked him, for the clamor aroused by the act makes me feel as if the act was necessary.' [2] Privately he realized his mistake and frankly admitted this to intimates. Nor did he ever repeat it. The aristocrat in Roosevelt was too convinced of his own standing to care about distinctions in others, but the politician in him understood the tactlessness of uselessly offending the prejudices of a great section of the country.

He was fond of the press and of the company of newspaper men, among whom he counted many warm friends. In the White House and afterward he confided in certain of these and rarely had occasion to regret his trust. The press in the United States occupies something of the position of an irresponsible parliament which offers an intermediary between the Administration and the public. Under our system of government there is no provision, such as exists in most European States, to ask or to answer questions on the floor of the legislative houses and two attempts made to authorize Cabinet officers to defend their measures before Congress have been unsuccessful. Roosevelt, who desired to find popular support for his policies, welcomed an agency like the press, which no one better than he knew how to utilize.

His methods of influencing opinion were at times undertaken with impish delight in his own humor. As he did not sympathize with Vice-President Fairbanks's ambition to succeed him, he felt intense pleasure when he discovered an opportunity to have cast on the latter a censorious ridicule because of the cocktail which the unfortunate Vice-President had been unwary enough to drink in his presence.

At a dinner of the Gridiron Club just before the end of the Administration, Fairbanks in his good-bye to the members said, perhaps recollecting the incident, that, although he had been frequently misunderstood, he had never 'thrown a line to trip an adversary.' When Roosevelt's turn to speak came, he remarked in his characteristic tone, 'The Vice-President says "he never threw a line to trip an adversary." In that he and I differ. I have thrown a line to trip an adversary, and — I would do it again.' [3]

Far more than Bryan, Roosevelt became a specialist in the American people. Bryan's strength arose from the fact that he belonged so completely to what a modern critic has termed the Genesis Belt. The hold he retained on its loyalty came through his ability to express its opinions and add convictions of moral fervor to advance personal interests. But Roosevelt, who on occasion would appear as orthodox as Bryan, could understand levels to which the latter would never have descended, and found elements of sympathy in slums and drawing-rooms as well as in farms and workshops.

He took enormous pains in securing the devoted loyalty of a body of followers scattered far and wide through the United States and engaged in the most varied occupations. They listened to him as their leader, primarily because he was their leader, and not because he was or had been President. No man in American life has ever been more persistent or industrious in his efforts to cultivate a wide circle of men who knew him personally. For years, deliberately, consciously, enjoyably, he had gone through the length and breadth of the country talking to people of every kind and occupation, but preferably to the lowly, mingling with mechanics, railway men, and miners. His personal acquaintance was enormous, his memory prodigious, his skill in bringing out his individuality in a variety of ways to the masses amounted to genius. The occupation of a lifetime, which at first seemed disconnected and purposeless, fitted in marvelously at the right moment. The labor of twenty years, which had long exposed him to the criticism and the ridicule of his own class, unable to understand what seemed to them at best an eccentricity, came like a swelling tide to lift him as a popular hero to the highest eminence.

He felt that he was in the White House not because of the politicians but in spite of them. The belief that he owed success to the hold he had on the people and the affection they bore him marked the real evolution of his character during his term of office. Before attaining the Presidency, he had thought that it would be possible to secure advancement only through the organization. Even when Governor of New York, the relations he had maintained with Platt had exposed him to much unfounded criticism. As President he discovered new strength. Although the politician in Roosevelt still occasionally resorted to methods which required his achievement to condone, there was another and greater Roosevelt beyond, imbued with a belief in himself as the chosen representative of the people, happy to fight their battle against the oppression of selfish interests. The dramatic instinct in his nature found satisfaction in the feeling that he, the champion of the plain people, had sprung from another lineage, that he had been nurtured in another environment which expected from him the defense of other interests. He came to believe in himself as the ordained chief who best understood the masses' aspirations, and whose mission it was by his leadership to bring the United States to a higher destiny. Interpreted in his own thought, his democracy flowed from the heart. When he took pleasure in singling out the virtues of the lowly, when he delighted in alluding to his personal friendship for men of humble circumstance and obscure walks of life, the inward thrill he felt at his ability to do this seemed also a tribute to the genuineness of his conviction. He admired in himself the chemist who had discovered new values in what before him had been regarded almost as waste products. The sense of dictatorship, unexpressed but latent within him and curbed by a higher sense of duty, was warranted in his eyes by the merit of all he represented, the patriotism of his intention and the provisional tenure of his power.

IV

No American has ever been elevated to the Presidency without his thoughts running to a second term, and Roosevelt would have been less than human had he failed in September, 1901, to think of the nomination three years later. Already, a month before McKinley's assassination, he had written to Lodge about his future. He had barely taken the oath of office when with characteristic emphasis he declared to a friend his intention to be full President, and his preference to be full President for three years rather than half President for seven years.

Since the Spanish War, Roosevelt's goal had been the Presidency in 1904. The tragic accident which

advanced him to the White House three years earlier
than he anticipated forestalled a result which had
become almost inevitable. Unlike most Vice-Presi-
dents who succeed, Roosevelt enjoyed a nation-wide
popularity except in the bosom of the Republican
organization. The Presidential nomination for this
reason contained at first an element of doubt. Already in the early days of his Administration a spat
with General Miles had caused him some apprehension over his prospects. In addition to several real or
supposed delinquencies, the General cherished the
further sin of Presidential ambitions. Roosevelt's
historian's instinct also discerned in Miles a supposed
resemblance to the notorious Wilkinson who com-
manded the Army under Jefferson, and there were
further imponderables which made for this dislike.
Roosevelt could never dislike without hating, or hate
without proclaiming failings on the part of his enemy
which called for the strongest public condemnation.
The consequence of this violent outburst was noticed
in States like Indiana, in which Miles enjoyed a
popularity so great that Roosevelt feared for a time
lest his own might have suffered beyond repair among
the Grand Army veterans.

The strange complex of the President's character
came out in the course of this incident. After he had
painted Miles publicly and privately in the blackest
colors, he felt that he might have gone too far. Had
he perhaps awakened one of those gusts of emotional
hysteria which occasionally sweep over America, as
uncontrollable as is the path of a tornado until it has
spent its force? He had aroused popular anger and

dreaded having overshot the mark. The nervous anxieties which inwardly troubled his mind never ruffled the surface. He only dug himself in and refused to retract, cost what it might, hoping that the folly of the Miles sympathizers would burn itself out. And at this stage of his career nothing seemed to hurt him.

Men in public life stand always at the crossroads between the wish to do and the fear over the consequences of their possible action. They hesitate without compelling reason to awaken a vindictiveness from those whose interests are disturbed, which may outlast the soon forgotten gratitude of the general public. Roosevelt at times was obsessed by this apprehension. His dramatic instinct always pictured his opponents as more dangerous than they really were. Under his seemingly impervious personality lay an acutely sensitive nervous nature. This came to the surface in the quickness of his response to suggestions, the crispness of his impressions, and the ability he displayed in detecting the more shadowy shapes of popular feeling often before these had risen above the surface. He was prone to exaggerate the ripples of criticism. The dangers he discerned never affected his outward countenance nor caused him, except over unimportant matters, to alter his line of conduct. But they left him with inward rackings, with intimate forebodings of impending disaster, and betrayed a very different Roosevelt from the buoyant optimist he always appeared to the public.

He knew when he had given offense, and measured the consequences in terms of political punishment. To his credit, he never hesitated in the face of

pressure which threatened him with defeat. Although
a deeper sagacity may have comforted him, his statement, that nothing would hire him to accept the
Presidency if he had to take it on terms which meant
the forfeiture of his own self-respect, was not far from
the truth. Underneath the politician in Roosevelt,
underneath the shallower and spectacular side which
his detractors stressed, underneath the playboy
instincts at which he himself could laugh, in the
deeper reaches of his soul, lay a sense of duty, which
at solemn moments caused him to act in a way to
justify the confidence reposed in him by millions of
his countrymen. Although ready to ask counsel of
many over the details of daily activity, when matters
of real moment arose there could be no other adviser
than his own conscience.

Roosevelt had begun his Presidency as only the
nominal head of the Republican Party, which was
still dominated by Hanna. Senator Hanna's influence
had been supreme in the McKinley Administration
and there was considerable speculation as to what his
relations would be with the new President. His early
estimate of Roosevelt had not been friendly. Hanna
had begun by opposing the nomination as Vice-President, and after the Philadelphia Convention he had
remarked to a friend that only one life stood between
the White House and that 'damned cowboy.' But
Hanna's attitude changed immediately when Roosevelt became President. He was shrewd enough and
generous enough to esteem his caliber, although the
two men always remained temperamentally far apart.
Personally liking the Senator, Roosevelt had no

intention of accepting his guidance. He had known him for a number of years and had begun by regarding him as a rough man, 'neither very far-sighted nor very broad-minded,' but shrewd, good-natured, and well-meaning.[4] Later his estimate of Hanna's abilities and appreciation of his loyalty grew considerably, but without rendering him more amenable to his influence. Hanna possessed a masterful personality which had ridden over many obstacles, and through his control of the party funds exercised a paramount influence on the questionable Republican organization in the Southern States. The custom had therefore grown up of consulting him over all Southern appointments and he expected the new President to acquiesce in this. To Hanna's astonishment, barely three weeks after Roosevelt became President, the latter, without asking him, appointed a liberal Democrat and an ex-Confederate as Judge of the United States District Court in Alabama. When the Senator wrote to ask the reason for this haste, Roosevelt frankly replied that experience taught him that in such cases a quick decision really prevented bitterness.

This incident, small in itself, illustrates admirably a number of different motives which, entirely distinct, yet came together to direct his judgment. A fortnight earlier, Roosevelt had told some Southern Congressmen who called on him to ask about his policy over appointments in the South that he intended to be President of the United States and not of any section, and that if he could not find the right Republicans to fill Southern places he proposed to appoint Democrats. The Alabama judgeship gave him a welcome opportunity to carry out these words and cut loose from both the disreputable Republican machine in the South and the undue influence of Senator Hanna, in a manner which he knew would enjoy the support of public opinion. Circumstances entirely dissociated in themselves coincided to bring about his decision.

The control of the organization still rested in Hanna's strong hands, and the latter's attitude toward the Presidency remained unknown, even though he did not seek the nomination for himself. He was then sixty-six years of age and in poor health. He knew that he would not make the best candidate, and party loyalty was always stronger in Mark Hanna than personal ambition. Behind him stood organized labor and organized capital, and he had received further offers of support from many quarters which placed him in a position of great strength toward Roosevelt. All the time Hanna's movements were being watched by the latter with suspicious apprehension. The Senator had begun by making a statement that he was not a candidate, had never been one, and would not be one, but finished by declaring that he was tired of going to the White House every day with his hand upon his heart. Intimates like William Loeb assured the President that Hanna would never make a fight, but Roosevelt remained unconvinced and regarded him as his only dangerous rival.

An incident occurred in Ohio between Foraker and Hanna which gave Roosevelt the opportunity to play his hand with superb skill. At the State Con-

vention in 1903, Senator Foraker had endorsed
Roosevelt for the Presidential nomination, probably
in order to embarrass Hanna and ingratiate himself
at the White House. Hanna telegraphed the same day
to the President to say that he had been obliged to
oppose this endorsement for reasons which he felt
convinced the latter would approve. Roosevelt's
answer was a masterpiece of dignified strategy. The
President declared that he had nothing to do with
raising the issue and had asked no one for his support. He found it only natural that those who favored
his nomination would support him and those who
opposed it would oppose him. Nothing could be
more elementary nor more subtle, for Hanna was
placed in the dilemma of having to show his hand
before the Convention, which he had done his best to
avoid, or opposing Roosevelt, which he was not prepared to do. Although the breach widened, it never
came to a head and a surface of friendly personal
relations was preserved. Hanna's death a few
months later, followed shortly by that of Senator
Quay, removed from the Republican organization
two outstanding and embarrassing personalities whose
ideas were poles apart from those of Roosevelt.

Men grow in importance both by their own achievement and by the disappearance of those who once
overtopped them. The country was already aware
that there was no one who measured up to Roosevelt
in stature, but the politicians had been slower to
recognize his merit. They were obliged to accept his
methods with grudging dislike, for automatically
Roosevelt had now become head of the organization.

It was only necessary for him to avoid conspicuous mistakes or giving offense in too many quarters in order to win.

To all except himself his nomination appeared to be a certainty and his election a foregone conclusion. The fighting spirit in his nature required, however, the sense of danger to arouse his pugnacity, in order to stir his best efforts. A deep grounded instinct felt the necessity of discovering something formidable in his adversary which others had failed to discern.

Alton B. Parker owed his nomination on the Democratic ticket to the hope of attracting the conservative vote and the support of the great financial interests. Few candidates have ever been more respectable or more colorless. His drab figure was then set against the most picturesque personality in American politics. The issue, as is often the case, was one of men and not of platforms. More and more our parties have come to resemble those vast convention halls in which they meet to perform the ceremonial of a venerable political liturgy. The process of reducing conflicting views or currents of opinion to their lowest denominator in order to make these acceptable to the greatest possible body of voters is one shared by both our great parties. Out of this stew of commonplace and compromise, cooked in a pale sauce and draped with the flag, there emerges the figure of the candidate, often swollen to inflated proportions. In the campaign of 1904 the struggle was uneven from the start. What could Alton B. Parker by any possibility suggest to the country in comparison with Theodore Roosevelt?

There was only one chance for Parker and only one danger existed for the Administration. Could the Democratic candidate exploit sufficiently the aversion of the financial interests to Roosevelt, and were these powerful enough to secure the latter's defeat? Would they be able or would they wish, with the great means at their disposal, to create a current against him throughout the country? Did they really prefer the conservative candidate of a radical party to the radical candidate of a conservative party?

Wall Street provides an easy formula of iniquity for millions in the United States. Men speak glibly of it in the way they do of the Roman Church, as though bankers welcomed the occasion to stake their influence in support of a supposed favorite. As a synthesis of the money interests of the country there exist within Wall Street too many rival ambitions and conflicting desires to find an easy unity. The Democratic leaders hoped to capitalize the indignation which Roosevelt's anti-trust measures had provoked, and obtain effective support from those financiers who openly professed to regard him as a dangerous lunatic. It is one thing to speak with violence when no responsibility is attached, and another to translate violent words into action and cash. Roosevelt, moreover, had numerous personal friends in Wall Street. Many, it is true, disliked him. But most of these proved that they were ready to swallow him in the same way as they had swallowed other things unpalatable to their taste. And the New York 'Sun' declared editorially in five words, 'Theodore with all thy faults,' that it stood behind him

IN THE CAMPAIGN OF 1904

Judge Parker's campaign began respectably enough with a courageous and politically sagacious advocacy of the gold standard which even alarmed Roosevelt into believing for a moment that he was confronted by a formidable adversary who, as he then remarked, had converted himself from a nobody into a somebody. Before long its promise petered out. Parker's speeches accusing Cortelyou, who was managing the campaign, with having used information gained while Secretary of Commerce and Labor to extort money for the party funds from the great corporations, drew from Roosevelt a carefully timed thunderbolt hurled at the most effective moment, three days before the election, when any retort, had even one been possible, would have wanted time to penetrate the voting mass. He pilloried Parker's statements as 'unqualifiedly and atrociously false.' Once more the piledriver almost wastefully crushed the gnat. Once more the President postured before the country as the strong man always able to pulverize his opponents.

The election proved a surprise only by the magnitude of the victory, which gave Roosevelt the largest vote in the electoral college and the largest popular majority that any candidate had ever recorded. The result far exceeded his most sanguine expectations. Previous moments of depression were forgotten amid the elation of triumph. At last his ambition of a lifetime was realized. He had become President in his own right.

V

Conversing one day with a distinguished British soldier who had visited him at Sagamore Hill, Roosevelt commented with biting irony on the difference between English and American methods of recognizing achievement, as illustrated by the Panama Canal. In England, he remarked, General Goethals would certainly have received a viscountcy, possibly an earldom, and Parliament would have voted him a large sum of money. In America, on the other hand, a Congressman from Iowa who had never before seen the sea would probably preside at the opening ceremonies of the Canal, at the same time that General Goethals might be at Washington undergoing a Congressional investigation.

Roosevelt regarded the Panama Canal as the crowning glory of his Administration. He ranked it with the Louisiana Purchase and the acquisition of Texas, and declared that, even if its price were to include his own elimination from politics, he would gladly pay this. The somewhat ostentatious pride he took was perhaps not entirely due to the achievement, but intended also to forestall the criticism which his act aroused. Attorney-General Knox's famous epigram, that so great an undertaking ought not to suffer from any taint of legality, expressed with caustic humor the misgivings aroused by Roosevelt's abrupt recognition of Panama after a revolution which he was charged with having fomented.

In his Message to Congress of January 4, 1904, Roosevelt made a spirited defense of his action, and fifteen years later he denounced as a 'Blackmail Treaty' the compensation which President Wilson recommended Congress to grant to Colombia. This consistent defense of his own policy over a long period of years was natural. He had always been determined not only to be right but to be righteous. The real problem of ethics presented by Roosevelt's part in the Panama Canal affair is one which concerns the philosophy of history more than it does the legal aspects of the transaction. Granting his character, his Western training, his steps to political success, and his admiration for English colonial methods, Roosevelt's conduct could not have been otherwise. Pragmatically, he realized that the justification for his action lay in its necessity and in its ultimate value.

The author of the 'Winning of the West' found in Panama a problem not unlike that which had confronted the early American settlers in Texas when their progress was impeded by the legal opposition of Mexico. He saw Colombia in possession of a strip of land with which she could do nothing, but the proper use of which was necessary to America and the world. Opinion at Bogota was then divided between the wish to utilize Panama as a pawn to obtain as high a price as possible and the reluctance of alienating Colombian soil in favor of an unwelcome neighbor like the United States. But Roosevelt discerned only the seamiest side of the Colombian attitude in refusing to ratify the Hay-Herran Treaty. He had never felt much respect for the Senators who opposed him at Washington. He had still less for those at Bogota. In common with other great men of decided opinions, he could discern only the vilest motives on the part of his opponents. Like his uncle, the former Confederate sailor who became an arch-Tory in England and regarded Gladstone as a man of exceptional infamy, Roosevelt also entertained the worst opinion of the Bogota politicians who had thwarted him. They were entitled to 'precisely the amount of sympathy we extend to other inefficient bandits,' he wrote to Cecil Spring Rice. To another friend he remarked that outside Turkey no more cruel despotism existed than that of the so-called Colombian Republic.

This feeling of contemptuous dislike provided the moral justification for Roosevelt's high-handedness. He found no reason to show further consideration because of abstract legal rights. The ambition to secure an enduring benefaction for the United States and the world, the love of achievement through action, the disgust for ineffectual wrangling with the Senate which he anticipated if the Panama route fell through, provided the motives which induced him to take lightning decisions unknown even to his Cabinet. In his own mind he was acting toward Colombia in the manner England had often acted toward lesser breeds. The 'white man's burden' was then ingrained in the political philosophy of the age and the white man in the White House was himself ready to assume any burden. Instinctively he justified his action by British precedent. It had been a good thing for Egypt and for India, he wrote, that England should be in control, and the same was true for the United States in Cuba and Panama. These countries appeared to

him to be our 'native States,' their Presidents were
our Khedives and our Rajahs. God's own Englishman
and God's own American could walk through the
world clasping hands.

Roosevelt was never greatly impressed by the
claims to sovereignty of the smaller republics in the
region bordering on the Caribbean though so long
as they behaved themselves he had no objection to
their managing their affairs. With a not unjustified
assumption of his own superiority, he refused to be
turned away from his great purpose by any obstacles
masquerading under a mere legal dress. But Roosevelt could not confine his task to being an empire-
builder. He had a more difficult work before him
than to justify his acts before an indulgent British
Colonial or Foreign Office whose main anxiety would
be in case a few cranks in Parliament refused to be
placated. Roosevelt knew that deep down among the
American people were qualms and questionings which
must be overcome. His battle had to be fought with
both an offensive and a defensive front. And he
found support and argument in Root and Hay, who
then dressed up to best advantage the legal and
diplomatic aspects of the affair. At first he thought
of proceeding with the Canal regardless of Colombian
rights and went so far as to prepare a message to
Congress to recommend this course. Wisely he abandoned the plan. He had found an ally in the French
bondholders, who had fallen into a state of consternation when they saw their hopes for compensation
dwindling to nothing between the action of the
Colombian Senate in rejecting the treaty and the fear

that the American Senate would revert to the Nicaraguan project and make their holdings valueless. Early in October of 1903, their representative, Mr. Bunau Varilla, called on Roosevelt in the White House. Exactly what was said at this interview has never transpired, but within a month the revolution at Panama broke out.

In a letter Roosevelt wrote to Dr. Albert Shaw, under date of October 10, 1903, which was intended for subsequent reference, he said: 'I cast aside the proposition made at this time to foment the secession of Panama. Whatever other governments can do, the United States cannot go into the securing by such underhand means the cession. Privately, I freely say to you that I would be delighted if Panama were an independent State, or if it made itself so at this moment; but for me to say so publicly would amount to an instigation of a revolt and therefore I cannot say it.' [5]

When the revolution broke out, Roosevelt denied emphatically that he had had anything to do with it. In his Message to Congress of January 4, 1904, he described the insinuations of governmental complicity as 'destitute of foundation as of propriety.... I think proper to say, therefore, that no one connected with this Government had any part in preparing, inciting, or encouraging the late revolution on the Isthmus of Panama.'

Hay, who probably ignored the details, characterized the affair as a 'perfect bit of honest statecraft.' Root with shrewd lawyer's instinct made a convincing case against the rights claimed by Bogota and the status of President Marroquin of Colombia. Roosevelt affirmed that his own part was that of a spectator. He had had nothing to do with the revolution and only knew what was common property. He had merely waited for events. From his own statement he had displayed an extraordinary forbearance. Under trying circumstances he himself did nothing except order our warships to be on the spot when the revolution he anticipated broke out.

It broke out at the most opportune moment. The unjust at Bogota were punished, the virtuous at Washington rewarded. It was all very simple, almost too simple. For the first time in his life, Roosevelt to all appearance had remained passive while the fate of what then was closest to his heart hung in the balance.

J. F. Rhodes, the historian, who knew Roosevelt well, approved of Senator Hanna's opinion that it would have been better to have exercised a little more patience. A question of tactics explains why this was undesirable. The Spooner Act stipulated that, if the President should be unable to obtain for the United States a satisfactory title to the property of the Panama Canal Company within a reasonable time and on reasonable terms, he might then fall back on the Nicaragua route. Roosevelt had good ground to be greatly opposed to the latter, but knowing the support this enjoyed in the Senate, which was to meet in December, he feared that the rejection by Bogota of the treaty negotiated for the Panama route would lead us back once more to Nicaragua.

Mr. Rhodes's guarded opinion does not attempt to

analyze the criticism aroused by Roosevelt's action. Three principal points are involved: The first concerns the charge of having fomented the revolt, which has not been proved, and which Roosevelt vigorously denied. The second was in opportunely ordering warships to the Isthmus whose presence stood in the way of Colombia reconquering her revolted province, but also prevented bloodshed and helped to restore an order which has since not been disturbed. The third was the over-hasty recognition of the new Republic, made necessary by the impending session of the Senate. If Roosevelt is to be condemned because of details still unrevealed, it becomes necessary also to condemn most of the processes which have made for security and progress in the backward regions of the world.

Roosevelt despised the wielder of power who was afraid to use his responsibility. In 1911, two years after he had ceased to be President, speaking at Berkeley, California, of the Panama Canal, he said: 'I took the Canal Zone and let Congress debate.' In his 'Autobiography' he wrote that he took it without even consulting his Cabinet, and in a speech delivered before the National Press Club in Washington on January 24, 1918, he explained that two courses lay open to him. He might have put the matter before the Senate, in which case there would have been half a century of discussion and perhaps the Panama Canal. Instead, he preferred to have the Panama Canal first and the half-century of discussion afterward. And he added humorously, 'Instead of discussing the Canal before it was built, which would have been harmful, they merely discuss me — a discussion which I regard with benign interest.' [6]

Although he condensed his action over Panama into the three words, 'I took it,' he was less indifferent to criticism than he admitted. Political instinct made him realize that to plunge into a maze of details would only weaken his case. He was ready to understand, even if he thought it foolish, the attitude of a man who preferred no canal rather than to have it built the way it was done. But he despised those who wanted the canal dug by a different process. Canal or no canal; there was the question which he put before the American people in its most rudimentary form. It had to be judged as a whole and not a hodgepodge of good and bad. If it was good, the steps necessary to build it must be good, and as he took the responsibility for these, he claimed the credit.

VI

The Presidency gave Roosevelt the opportunity, in handling questions of foreign policy, to reveal the only side of his talents which he himself may previously not have suspected. His success as a diplomatist came from combining the skill of a politician and the learning of an historian with the principle of a cowboy never to draw his gun unless prepared to shoot. The impression of resolution which by these means he attached to foreign policy raised the prestige of the United States to a height it had never before attained.

The Roosevelt touch may be discerned as much in his diplomacy as in his political methods. When a

situation shaped itself clearly in his mind, he ap-
praised the means at his disposal and then hit just as
hard, as swiftly, and as quietly, as he could. The
only difference lay in the silencer which he attached
to his diplomacy and his readiness to conceal personal success by lavishing praise on the other side.
A spat with the Kaiser over Venezuela in December,
1902, which many years afterward reached the public
ear, illustrates this technique. Under President
Cleveland a controversy of similar nature with Great
Britain occasioned some hot messages to Congress,
and brought the two nations to the verge of war at
a time when our navy was well nigh non-existent.
It would be unfair to assume that the easy popularity
which any administration can acquire by a spirited
defense of the elastic Monroe Doctrine entered into
Cleveland's reasoning. But Roosevelt has often been
charged with maneuvering for popularity and it
would be hard to find a more convincing illustration
of his readiness to forgo this at a time when it lay
within his grasp. Cleveland's threat remained written on paper, but Roosevelt then held in his hand the
only real argument which the Kaiser could understand. Yet he did not ask for support, nor excite
national feeling, nor take Congress into his confidence
by calling its attention to the consequences of a German occupation of a Venezuelan port close to the
future Panama Canal.

Not half a dozen men in the United States then
knew that Admiral Dewey, who had been dispatched
to Porto Rico with fifty ships of war, ostensibly for
maneuvers, carried peremptory orders to keep these

in fighting trim ready to sail at a moment's notice. Although Roosevelt was determined to prevent the German naval force from taking possession of any Venezuelan territory, even Admiral Dewey himself did not know what was then in the President's mind. When Dr. von Holleben, the German Ambassador, declared at the White House that his Government refused the President's suggestion to arbitrate, Roosevelt replied that he would wait another ten days for this at the end of which he would order Dewey to the Venezuelan coast. The Ambassador expressed consternation at the consequences of such an order, and Roosevelt with intimate knowledge of the superiority at that time of our navy to the German, pointed to the map to show him that, in the event of a conflict with the United States, Germany would nowhere be at a greater disadvantage than in the Caribbean. A few days later, when the Ambassador, who had called at the White House, indicated that arbitration would not be entertained, Roosevelt remarked that in that event it was useless to wait the ten days and Dewey would receive his orders to sail twenty-four hours sooner. A press dispatch from Washington on December 18 had reported that our fleet would assemble at Trinidad off the coast of Venezuela. The next day the German Emperor accepted the principle of arbitration, which, to make a graceful amend, he requested Roosevelt himself to undertake. As the latter declined, the case was referred to the Hague Tribunal. No explanation was given about the reason for the sudden reversal of the German attitude, but Dr. von Holleben soon

after was recalled to Berlin in disgrace. The dis-
comfiture of the Kaiser over Venezuela, carefully
hidden under words of praise for his acceptance of the
principle of arbitration, undoubtedly increased the
latter's admiration for Roosevelt. The complete
silence maintained by the President on this occasion
allayed any sting.

Success in life had been bound up in Roosevelt's
mind with a philosophy of action which he applied
with marked results to foreign policy. He enjoyed
nothing more keenly than coupling deeds to words
and utilizing the fleet as a working adjunct to his
diplomacy. The impression of quick strength which
only a navy can produce without real risk of war gave
mathematical demonstration to his words and made
diplomacy partake of the nature of an exact science.
The famous voyage of the fleet around the world,
which many at first regarded with misgiving, became
an impressive demonstration of the new strength of
America which he personally had done so much to
build up.

He had blamed the boorish tactics employed at
San Francisco toward Japanese school-children and
lavished fulsome praise on Japan, with whose injured pride he sympathized. It was one thing to scold
Californians and another to deprive them of their
right to legitimate protection. The irritation underlying our relations with Japan had left an angry
situation brewing underneath, which might become
dangerous through any suspicion of weakness. Roosevelt's instinct led him to balance the domestic rebuke
he administered in San Francisco with an outward

demonstration of strength in which the entire country could take pride. To defend California he welcomed an opportunity to utilize his long-standing interest in the Navy and show Japan that our preparedness was covered with a smile.

The most pugnacious of our Presidents by persuading two continents of his earnestness served the cause of peace. Roosevelt was rarely hasty over controversies when he himself understood that these comported real risk. The effective way in which, through a personal letter he addressed to Justice Holmes, then in London, the latter advised Joseph Chamberlain of the strong views the President held regarding the Alaska Boundary Dispute and his refusal to submit this controversy to arbitration in case of a deadlock, was a masterpiece of secret diplomacy entirely beneficent in its purpose. The victory obtained through Lord Alverstone, the English member of the Commission, casting his vote with the American delegates upon the only important point in the controversy, was a personal triumph for Roosevelt. The steps he had taken to facilitate this result remained for years hidden from public knowledge.

Certain of his letters illustrate admirably his own ideas as to the limitations of his action. He wrote to Spring Rice about the situation in the Far East that it would be well-nigh impossible even if it were not undesirable for the United States to engage with another country 'to carry out any policy save one which had become part of the inherited tradition of the country like the Monroe Doctrine.' It would be necessary to reckon with defeat in Congress, with

popular temper, and with many different conditions.
'In consequence my policy must of necessity be
somewhat opportunist.' [7] For similar reasons Roosevelt frankly declared that he would hesitate to count
on the support of the British Government or people.
He did not feel convinced about their tenacity of
purpose or willingness to take risks or endure losses
for a given end. In last analysis no nation can depend
upon the friendship of another unless it has itself such
strength as to make its own amity of value in return.
As things stood in the world, no state could rely on
inoffensiveness for safety nor on alliance with any
other nation to achieve security. His own purpose
was 'to keep America in trim so that fighting her
shall be too expensive and dangerous a task to likely
be undertaken by anybody.' At the same time he intended to make her act in a spirit of justice and good
will toward others so as to prevent any one from
lightly taking this risk.[8]

Full of resourcefulness and persistent in his ideas,
he was not obstinate about his methods. When the
so-called 'Protocol' to cover our protectorate over
San Domingo failed in the Senate, he presented the
matter session after session, under different designations, until the wearied Senators ratified the agree-
ment. This persistency tired out his adversaries and
the success he met with enhanced his prestige for
achievement. The impression of vigor he created
extended to every continent. The sheer force of his
determination, the ingrained belief in his readiness to
back his word, proved to be the most powerful asset
of his time toward keeping the peace. He would never

have allowed the country to slip into war through
indecision.

The President, inclined by temperament and philosophy to quick action, did not always take sufficient
regard of the risk he incurred by his decisions. At
least in two instances he took measures which, unknown to the country, and at first unsuspected by
himself, exposed him to considerable danger. The extraordinary prestige attached to his name abroad,
even in remote regions, made for his success. The cry
of 'Perdicaris alive or Raisuli dead,' in the case of a
naturalized citizen, of somewhat questionable status,
kidnaped in Morocco, thrilled America by its picturesque appeal. Perdicaris's safe return from Raisuli's
brigand lair brought a difficult situation to a fortunate
end. Otherwise, the possibility of American marines
being obliged to scour the Moorish mountains or seize
the Tangier customs, at a time when that land had
already become a football for dangerous international
politics, might have added an intolerable strain to a
most irritating situation.

The false report of the murder of an American Vice-
Consul at Beirut provoked an unnecessarily hasty
order given at the White House, unknown even to
John Hay, for an American squadron to sail at once to
Syrian waters. This excursion of an armed force in
the Near East proved highly embarrassing to Mr.
Leishman, then our envoy at Constantinople, who
felt nervous lest a European veto be placed on our interference. The fact that such apprehension led to no
further consequence is a tribute to Roosevelt's prestige and confirmed him in his audacity, without

American opinion realizing the risk taken. When on a later occasion he dispatched a squadron to Smyrna, the immediate effect of this order was to attain at least a paper settlement of several long-standing litigious questions between Turkey and the United States.

It has erroneously been said that Roosevelt in his more delicate negotiations preferred to utilize foreign envoys like Jusserand and Speck because of their superior training. The reason was different. Both were warm friends, and at times he conducted important matters through them, unknown even to his Secretary of State. He did this, perhaps, to avoid embarrassing records which the Senate might ask for, and also because of the enjoyment he felt in personally handling a delicate international negotiation. He was on even more intimate terms with Spring Rice, who had been his best man at his wedding in London, and who was one of the small coterie at Washington which included Lodge and Henry Adams. Roosevelt and Spring Rice, both with sharp tongues and irascible natures, had many a spat together in the days when the former was still a Civil Service Commissioner and the latter a Second Secretary. But their friendship never wavered and all through life Spring Rice corresponded on intimate terms with Roosevelt. He was at times an invaluable secret informant to the most autocratic of Presidents. The unfavorable opinion which he, as an English diplomatic secretary, expressed of one American Ambassador led to the latter's transfer.[9] It would be difficult to find a parallel instance in modern times

where the Chief of a great State should have maintained a political correspondence of a highly confidential nature, in which he expressed himself freely
and disparagingly about other friendly nations, with
a subordinate official in the service of a foreign
country.

Roosevelt felt ample confidence in his own capacity
for directing foreign affairs. Yet he appreciated Hay,
and more especially Elihu Root, both of whom were
admirable public servants and his devoted friends.
John Hay, high-minded, but a cultivated skeptic at
heart, was satisfied to remain in the State Department
without giving forceful expression to his opinions,
and only when solicited, offered his always excellent
advice. He cared neither to wrangle with the Senate
nor with the President. His judgment was ripe, his
experience rich, his methods statesmanlike, but he
was neither insistent on pressing for his own point of
view nor was he always consulted by Roosevelt.

The President utilized his authority in a useful
manner to remedy many of the shortcomings caused
by an inadequate diplomatic service which reflected
the country's long lack of interest in foreign affairs.
There had been little or no relation between the
growing strength of the Nation and the inadequate
nature of our representation in foreign lands, disguised under the self-deceptive plea of a disinterested
aloofness which no longer corresponded with the
facts. The price of regarding diplomatic posts, not
as a means for expressing American interest abroad,
but as the reward for service at home, is in the nature
of a Subsidy granted to the President for his own

purposes and has unconsciously been paid by the
Nation in the scanty return received from its foreign
policy. The foundations of what was intended to
become a permanent diplomatic career in the United
States built from the bottom were then laid by Roosevelt's efforts. He took a keen personal interest in
appointments, and, though keeping in mind political
considerations, he raised the selection of our repre-
sentatives to a high standard which subjected even
the smallest posts to his close scrutiny. On one
occasion, having named an admittedly unsatisfactory
candidate to a minor diplomatic secretaryship, he
humorously explained the nomination by saying that,
as his choice lay between granting this and murdering
the applicant's mother who had pestered him with
excessive perseverance, he preferred the lesser evil.

The steps which give rise to official dignities in the
United States are often more easily rushed than they
can be climbed. Power in American political life is
still too personal, and there hardly exists, as in the
countries of Western Europe, a strong, half-anony-
mous bureaucracy, seated amid deep-grown respect,
with venerable traditions behind it, which is able to
restrain executive appointments. The term of a
presidential administration marks so brief a period in
the Nation's life that it seems natural for a strong
President to elevate to high distinction those in whom
he places confidence. Whoever, then, in the Government service met with Roosevelt's favor, enjoyed a
meteoric career. There was no stagnation in the ranks,
for the President infused his own quick energy into
all those around him.

The inadequate appreciation given to Roosevelt's diplomatic talents illustrates a common discrepancy between popular estimate and reality. In his accepted portrait the features of a diplomat are left unlimned. The emphasis laid on his more picturesque aspects has pushed into the shade occasions in which his skill was no less because success required silence. A paradox may seem to exist between Roosevelt the taciturn and Roosevelt taking the people into his confidence with all the publicity of which he was master. This contradiction is more apparent than real. The President's diplomatic achievements contained at least as much of the spectacular as characterized his other public acts. That he avoided all semblance of sensation and even hid his results was due to no ambiguity of character, but only to a difference of technique, calculated in each case to serve its purpose. The appeal to the sensational in Roosevelt has erroneously been regarded as an inherent trait in his nature instead of a method meant only to attain a deliberate purpose. No more convincing proof of this can be offered than the complete secrecy which attended his most important diplomatic negotiations. Only many years later, the publication of confidential documents, which by that time had become history, has revealed how steps taken on his sole initiative preserved the world's peace. The enormous prestige he enjoyed among statesmen was gained by a series of successes in international affairs which deservedly earned this for him, although the most important of his triumphs were known to very few.

The silence with which his negotiations were conducted offers the best rejoinder to such absurdities as the wholesale condemnation of so-called secret diplomacy which, with confused thought, brands indiscriminately methods with results. Had Roosevelt's diplomacy been public, had he taken the world into his confidence on the occasions when he out-maneuvered the Kaiser, he would never have scored his success and might have caused untold harm. If questions affecting national pride and concealing underneath personal ambition and vanity are publicly to be threshed out on all occasions and in every phase of their negotiation, the addition of such complications will only mean further elements of discord with which to embitter international controversy. It was Roosevelt's merit disinterestedly to have put aside the popular applause to which he was entitled and which he loved, and to have chosen instead the silent settlement of grave diplomatic problems.

When Roosevelt was trying to obtain English assistance in order to bring pressure on Japan to end the war, he wrote Spring Rice, who had reminded him of the British treaty obligation not to allow a hostile combination against Japan, that he also, as soon as hostilities broke out, had notified Germany and France 'in the most polite and discreet fashion' that in the event of a combination against Japan to try to do what Russia, Germany, and France did to her in 1894, he would promptly side with Japan and proceed to whatever lengths were necessary in her behalf. He knew that England would stand by him because of her alliance, but thought it best that there should be no previous consultation before announcing his purpose.¹⁰ The fact that he alone could have committed the United States to a course of action which conceivably might have led to a world conflagration is so remarkable that it would be surprising if Roosevelt's step had been more than a verbal hint dropped to the French and German Ambassadors, with both of whom he was on intimate terms.

Roosevelt followed the progress of the war with keen interest. His impression of events in Russia was largely inspired by Spring Rice, who as Counselor of the British Embassy at Petrograd wrote at great length to Mrs. Roosevelt what he wanted the President to know. English interests for peace in the Far East coincided with our own, and the opportunity soon arose for Roosevelt to act the welcome part of a peacemaker a year after the possibility of utilizing his good offices had first been broached by the Japanese.¹¹ The opportunity was more than welcome to the President, but he approached his task with his customary attention to the minutest detail while resorting to the most unconventional methods.

On July 17, 1905, the eve of the Russo-Japanese Peace Conference, Roosevelt wrote to J. St. L. Strachey, editor of the London 'Spectator,' that the Russians having been entirely unable to make war seemed entirely unable to make peace and stupidly unwilling to face the fact that they were at their opponent's mercy. 'Entirely for your information I wish to say that I undertook these negotiations only at the request of Japan.' ¹²

It is somewhat unusual to find the head of a State writing to a foreign journalist in a foreign country, expressing his outspoken opinion in so disparaging a manner about a great power, on the eve of a delicate diplomatic negotiation which he had just taken a leading part in bringing about. To the credit of Roosevelt's judgment of men, this confidence was not misplaced and no embarrassment was suffered from his frankness. His reason for then writing to Strachey was probably attributable neither to any particular intimacy nor to inexperience or accident. Roosevelt, though often giving a casual semblance to his acts, rarely did anything haphazardly. The writer, for instance, has in his possession a lengthy letter Roosevelt addressed to him on a later occasion, which contains a highly adverse opinion of another English journalist whom he disliked, presumably written solely with a view to its being shown to the editor of a periodical in which articles by the writer had appeared. When Roosevelt wrote with such frankness to Strachey, doubtless he wanted to secure his assistance with the English Press in the forthcoming negotiations between Russia and Japan. Hitherto he had obtained little support from the British Government in persuading its Japanese ally to make peace. Certain expressions convinced him that the opinion was current in England that his own action for peace had been undertaken at the instance of the Czar. He therefore desired a prominent English editor, in whose discretion he relied, to know that he had begun these negotiations 'only' at the request of Japan and that his personal opinion of the Russians was highly unfavorable. After this he anticipated that Strachey would find little difficulty in persuading influential British journalists that Roosevelt was in no way pro-Russian as had been alleged, and that his action had been prompted by Japan. This letter illustrates the care with which a seeming indiscretion was intended to serve a definite purpose.

The minute attention he paid to trifles with which a Chief of State would normally not concern himself can also be judged from the personal care he exercised when receiving the Russian and Japanese delegations on the Mayflower. On that occasion he showed himself not only a host, but a master of ceremonies. When luncheon was announced, he led the envoys into the saloon in such a way that no one could notice who went first. Purposely there were no chairs around the luncheon table and consequently no question of precedence was raised. When at the end of the repast he proposed an appropriate toast, he requested that it be drunk in silence and that there should be no reply.

His mothering of the Peace Conference at Portsmouth was continuous, persuasive, irresistible. To the Czar he offered 'advice which he would have given him were he a Russian patriot and statesman,' just as two months earlier he had written the Kaiser as to Morocco to say that no consideration would make him give counsel against his interest or honor. Yet his real opinion of both during all this time when he was acting the Russian patriot and the German counselor was most unflattering. 'The more I see of the Czar, the Kaiser, and the Mikado, the better content I am with democracy, even if we have to include the American newspaper,' he wrote to Lodge.

He felt amused by the English belief that he was
under the Kaiser's influence in undertaking the
negotiations. 'The heavy-witted creatures do not
understand that nothing would persuade me to follow
the lead or enter into close alliance with a man who
is so jumpy, so little capable of continuity of action,
and therefore so little capable of being loyal to his
friends or steadfastly hostile to an enemy.' [13] At a
time when the Kaiser was at the height of his fame,
this opinion is not without relish.

He took occasion to sermonize Japan, filled with
pride at her newly acquired position among nations,
over the duties she also owed the world. As soon as
war or peace hinged solely on her ability to collect
an indemnity, Roosevelt stigmatized the unworthi-
ness of pecuniary motives for continuing hostilities.
In the end his tact, his driving power, and his courage
triumphed over every obstacle and brought the
thorny peace negotiations to a successful conclusion.
Congratulations were showered on him by crowned
heads and he received the most cordial thanks both
from the Czar and the Emperor of Japan.

His head was not turned by the applause. To his
daughter Mrs. Longworth he could write of the sar-
donic amusement he derived at his work being over-
valued merely because it had succeeded. 'If I had
not brought about peace, I should have been laughed
at and condemned. Now I am overpraised.' In the
moment of his success he thought, half humorously
and half bitterly, of the long years of struggle he had
gone through, of the ridicule he had encountered, and
the isolation he had endured. His attempt to reform

New York politics, he then recalled, had been far
more arduous than urging two warring but exhausted
nations together. The philosophy of his life stands
out better in his refusal to be carried away by success
than in the platitudinous sermons he enjoyed preaching. There is merit in the belief that the reward of
action lies not in victory, but in action well done.
At the time when the praise of the world was lavished
upon him, he wrote to his brother-in-law Douglas
Robinson: 'Don't be misled by the fact that just at
the moment men are speaking well of me. They will
speak ill soon enough.'

The Moroccan question brought the Kaiser and
Roosevelt together in an even more curious way.
Doubtless the principle of the 'open door' which
John Hay had successfully maintained in China was
not foreign to the Emperor's original idea. The latter
was obsessed by the fear of 'encirclement' and the
wish to score. Why could not the 'open door' in
Morocco also be utilized as a leverage to induce
American support to balance the British assistance
to France? It was reasonable to suppose that a
statesman with the aggressive personality of Roosevelt might welcome an opportunity to assert in
Morocco, with German aid, the same principle which
we had struggled for successfully in China.

The events which led up to the Moroccan Conference at Algeciras were the first prelude to the
Great War. How near it was to breaking out may be
judged by the Emperor's communications to Roosevelt in which he affirmed that only if he were to
receive no support from the interested treaty powers

to keep the 'open door' would he then be obliged 'to choose between the possibility of a war with France and the examining of those conditions which France may have to propose so as to avoid a war.' The Kaiser tried to secure the President's assistance on the plea that this should be rendered in order to avoid a war. But Roosevelt was too wary to fall into this trap and replied frankly that he disliked taking a position in any matter unless he intended to back it up. American interests in Morocco were not sufficiently great to warrant entangling the Government. The Kaiser reverted to the likelihood of war even after the French had endeavored to pacify him by offering Germany a sphere of interest in Morocco. The memorandum which he sent to Roosevelt contained the ominous words, 'We may be forced into war not because we have been *grabbing* after people's land, but because we *refuse to take it.*'

After this Roosevelt urged France to accept the idea of a conference on the ground that it would make more difficult an unprovoked attack by Germany. He sent word to the French that he would 'if necessary take very strong grounds against any attitude of Germany which seemed to him unjust and unfair.' When France agreed to accept his advice, Roosevelt wrote at once to congratulate the Emperor on 'a diplomatic triumph of the first magnitude.'

Six months more of haggling between France and Germany were still necessary, during which Roosevelt was obliged to put forward compromise suggestions. The Moroccan Conference met at last at Algeciras in January, 1906, and three months later a treaty was drawn up which was also signed by the two American delegates, Henry White, then our Ambassador to Italy, and J. R. Gummere, our representative in Morocco.

The writer was Secretary of the American Delegation at the Algeciras Conference. All the telegraphic and written dispatches passed through his hands and the cipher was in his care. He still recalls his own amazement as a young diplomatist at finding that a Conference on which the gaze of the world was fixed, and which had been attended by men of real or supposed eminence occupying the highest dignities in their respective countries, should after three months of deliberation only have been able to achieve the most mediocre results. He knew nothing at the time or till long afterward of the antecedent steps which Roosevelt had taken in arranging that the Conference should meet, or the important part he had performed in persuading the French to accept the proposal on the ground that it would work out to their advantage, or in inducing the Kaiser to recede from his original position which threatened war. He is convinced that Mr. Gummere also knew nothing of what Roosevelt's part had been, and he later ascertained that Mr. White was equally innocent and only informed after it was over. In other words, one of Roosevelt's most important accomplishments was carried out unknown to the agents he himself had appointed to represent the United States in the international conference that emanated from his work. He deliberately eschewed the applause which by every right should have been given him for his unceasing labor to save the peace of

Europe.   After the Conference had been successfully
terminated, he chronicled the various steps he had
taken which led to this result in a confidential letter
to Mr. Reid, our Ambassador in London, to serve for
his information and to preserve for history the record
of his achievement.

The effusive praise which Roosevelt lavished on the
Kaiser in the course of these negotiations was characteristic of his method. Officially he appealed to the
Emperor's 'fame in history' and to the sincere
admiration he entertained for him. In a private letter
to Taft, he wrote that 'the Kaiser's pipe-dream this
week takes the form of Morocco.' The flattery was
more than justified, when the Emperor directed his
Ambassador at Washington to say at the White
House that if, at the Conference, differences of opinion should arise between France and Germany, he
would always be ready to accept Roosevelt's decision.

Alone, unaided, and unsuspected, Roosevelt in the
Moroccan crisis gave the measure of his diplomatic
skill. Congress knew nothing, the country knew
nothing, his own agents knew nothing, the world
knew nothing, of all he had done to preserve peace.
A President more imbued with a fundamentalist
attitude toward diplomacy would have taken refuge
in American lack of interest in European questions
and have refused to meddle in its affairs. A President
of lesser caliber might have utilized the vast organs
of publicity at his disposal to impress the world with
the full value of his accomplishment. The gentleman
and the statesman in Roosevelt preserved his modesty and left his achievement for a later generation

to appraise, while he obtained his satisfaction from
the knowledge of having helped to keep peace. He
had played a magnificent game with two friends like
Jusserand and Speck, the French and German
Ambassadors, both of whom he genuinely liked and
trusted. The game was how to handle the Kaiser, the
stake was the world's peace, and Roosevelt won.
He asked nothing more. His steps were not particularly subtle nor deep. They were the obvious intelligent steps which a capable man of experience, tact,
and good intention, occupying a commanding position, courageous and confident in himself, unafraid
of responsibility, and above all a gentleman at heart,
would have taken, for only a gentleman would afterward have kept silence. They were taken disinterestedly and almost playfully, with keen enjoyment.
The playboy in Roosevelt joined with the statesman
and the diplomatist in securing the peace of the world.

VII

Roosevelt felt unbounded admiration for Lincoln.
Few characters could be more unlike and yet by
different processes both had sought the same goal.
He envied Lincoln's nearness to the plain people and
the instinctive and almost mystic sense of his leadership. He knew that neither by mere words nor by
intellectual abstractions could he approach the
intimacy of Lincoln's communion with the people.
The depth of his feeling could not be simulated.
Roosevelt was deficient in emotional sentiment of this
nature. His affections were strong but intensely
personal and confined almost solely to his own family.

It is difficult for any man in public life to preserve for
long a sensitive feeling toward others. The edge of
keenness is apt to wear off, even though he finds ready
substitutes for this in rhetorical devices. Roosevelt's
kinship with the plain people was less near than
Lincoln's, his affection was less deep, but his zeal
was greater and more practically directed than had
been possible during the Civil War. The difference
in character could also be measured by the difference
in method of the two Presidents.

Roosevelt took only a secondary interest in workmen's struggles for shorter hours and higher wages.
This was a material side of their welfare which he
approved of, but which did not particularly appeal
to him. Labor questions touched him more nearly
when they formed part of what he regarded as the
real interests of the plain people. The sympathy
which twenty years earlier he had expressed in the
Assembly at Albany for the dwellers of New York
slums was now reawakened. It touched his activity
in the White House and he felt a response to his
solicitude all the more pleasing, as it seemed to reach
him undefiled, straight from the wells of popular
approval. Later, when no longer President and unrestrained by office, he felt increasingly that his greatest task in life was to be the people's champion and
there grew in his mind a deep-grained belief in this
Messianic mission which was to overweight his
judgment. But the Presidential office exercised a
sobering restraint, even on Roosevelt, for preferences
had there to be translated into terms of official
appointment and legislative enactment. The political

mysticism he afterward displayed was at this time
still undeveloped. In its place the pressure of circumstances of a different nature forced him to consider the network of problems grouped together under
the general label of labor, and which revolved around
the recognition of unions and the regulation of
salaries and work.

Roosevelt's attitude toward the working man was
contained in loudly repeated formulas of democracy,
square deal, and Americanism. As general proposi-
tions these were indisputable and they allowed him
to recommend several practical measures of social
legislation. The human side of these appealed to his
sense of justice, the wisdom of possessing a contented
working class appealed to him as a statesman, the
expediency of enacting proper labor laws appealed
to him as a politician. This was not all. Years before,
when still a youngster, Roosevelt had been dubbed
the 'scholar in politics,' at a time when a standard
bordering on illiteracy was not far remote from the
lower reaches of our political life. In the stricter
sense of the word Roosevelt was no scholar, but his
reading at all times was extensive and assiduous.
He had been keenly interested in measures of social
welfare taken by different European countries under
the general designation of 'state socialism.' He knew
that the nations of Western Europe were more advanced than the United States in regulating questions
such as child labor, providing maternity benefits,
and workmen's compensation for injury. At a time
when few practical politicians in America had yet
heard of this, Roosevelt was familiar with the pro-

gramme of social legislation abroad, which was attempting to alleviate the misery caused by sickness,
unemployment, and indigent old age.

Measures of this character instinctively appealed
to his sympathy. Among other benefits he appreciated the additional power conferred on the organs of
the State as a beneficent medium competent to redress the grosser abuses inherent in our industrial
system. Cynical observers who watched Roosevelt's
interest in social welfare gave him no further credit
than that of seeking the political benefit to be derived. They maligned him in this, as mistaken in
their prejudice as were those who, persuaded only of
his virtues, deemed it unworthy of their hero to enter
into such calculations. Ingrained in Roosevelt there
came out the country squire, modernized and magni-
fied, conforming himself to present-day conditions
and changing his benevolent interest from tenants
and farmhands to workmen in the factories and
dwellers in the slums.

A semi-feudal relation still prevails in our politics.
It is intangible and hard to define, but it permeates
the structure of the organization and no one appreciated its significance better than Roosevelt, both
when it opposed him and when he felt able to command its loyalty. The mechanics and the railway
men who supported him enthusiastically were, in a
political sense, his retainers. They offered him their
allegiance and he gave them his service. Deliberately
he attempted to establish a new kind of relation between the State and the various groups who together
form the plain people. He wanted these to realize the

solicitude he felt for their welfare and to help them in their citizenship. The State in his mind was no mere anonymous and impersonal expression of the Nation, but a sentient and human creation over which he presided with magnificent and benevolent energy.

A coal strike which threatened to disrupt the life of a huge section of the country at the outset of his Administration brought him face to face with dangerous labor troubles. The President's right of interference in a private dispute was questionable. Conservative opinion resented the attempt, and his mediation was undesired by the operators, who thought they had found in the strike an opportunity to crush the unions. A series of steps which Roosevelt took almost haphazardly, aided by Root, who remained in the background, ended in a settlement which came at the most opportune time. The result conferred on the President a deserved prestige to reward him for the grave risk assumed. He kept silence over other measures then in his mind to use in case the negotiations had failed and which contemplated a kind of military receivership for the coal mines, easier to introduce than to terminate. Fortunately there was no need for him to resort to such risky experiments.

Roosevelt has left a humorous description of the conference in the White House at which the eventual settlement of this strike was arranged. The drama which had seemed imminent ended in a comedy, when the labor representative at his suggestion was turned into an eminent sociologist to placate the coal owners into accepting him as an arbitrator. His own sympathy lay with the miners, partly because he liked their leader, John Mitchell, and even more because he disliked the coal owners, who combined pharisaical virtue with an offensive truculence. Wall Street gave out that Roosevelt was entirely on the labor side and prepared to make war on capital. It was currently said that he would not treat working men in the same way that he would treat capitalists if the former violated the law.

Roosevelt maintained that he was President neither of labor nor of capital, but of the American people, and that his duty was to enforce the law. He assumed toward the unions the same balanced attitude as toward the trusts. Labor also, he proclaimed, had its good and bad sides and unions could be either useful or pernicious. They formed part of the evolution of industry as much as the corporations, and like the latter ought also to be restrained when they acted illegally. Roosevelt's refusal to pander to the improper demands of the unions became conspicuous when he ordered the reinstatement in the Government Printing Office of Miller, a typesetter who had been discharged only because of having been expelled from his union. This issue arose at an awkward moment before the election when he risked alienating many votes and pressure was brought to bear on him. But in such cases pressure aroused his fighting instinct. Nothing made him so determined as a threat. The courage and independence he displayed was also political wisdom, for the impression he made on the public, as he well knew, was based on confidence in his possessing precisely these virtues. Although he

was applauded at the time, the political skepticism
which always lay deep beneath the skin of his boisterous self-confidence caused him to feel misgivings. He
feared, though mistakenly, lest the country would
forget all about the incident, 'while the labor men
who are angry will not forget.' The patriot in Roosevelt never misled him into cherishing unduly favorable estimates of his own countrymen.

He followed a middle course toward labor. Habits
of balanced reasoning acquired many years earlier
caused him to state every question in terms of elementary morality in order to appeal to the understanding of the great body of the electorate. His
solemnly asserted pronouncements that right was
right and wrong was wrong, of justice for all and
the necessity of punishing evil-doers, high or low,
covered a not infrequent uncertainty about the procedure to adopt and a consequent moderation in
the measures recommended. The obviousness of the
truths he enunciated once caused Tom Reed to chaff
Roosevelt about having rediscovered the Ten Com-
mandments. He was too shrewd not to appreciate
that the mere statement of such commonplaces without otherwise enlivening them by apt illustrations
would bore the people. Eternal truths had to be
brought to date to make them effective. He applied
moral points to condemn well-known personalities.
A list of undesirable citizens was extended to include
labor agitators, whose names were publicly pilloried
along with those of the best-known Wall Street
financiers. Moyer and Heywood, accused of murder
in Idaho, were associated in the same breath with

Harriman, with whom Roosevelt had been on friendly terms. His pronouncements, almost in the form of syllogisms, stigmatized his enemies in order to prove moral conclusions.

Such tactics were absurdly simple, yet they have remained inimitable to this day. Originality lay in the method of their presentation and the vivid interpretation he gave. His statements, delivered with a newspaperman's crispness and a boxer's punch, never failed to command public attention. Far more than a mere President, he was, then, the real leader of the country. He had captured the conservative Republican Party and injected new life into it. The interest he took in social questions gave a novel direction to American politics which may be felt increasingly in the future. Many followed him then out of loyalty, believing rather in his star than having confidence in his cause. Old-time politicians snarled. Some of them regarded Roosevelt as a madman, but they knew that he was too strongly entrenched in the country's affection to be overthrown.

VIII

The true significance of the 'trusts' which characterized the early years of the century had not at once been understood. Their sudden growth meant more than an economic and a social phenomenon. The formation of great corporations with a centralized direction over productive activities had become inevitable in a land without real barriers, inhabited by a people energetic, resourceful, and homogeneous in their economic wants. Along with common

political institutions and language, the mechanical
processes of transportation and manufacturing helped
to unify a continent and bring an increasing standard-
ization into American life.

Instead of introducing economic feudalism, as
some then erroneously alleged, the new direction
pointed toward a kind of industrial absolutism which
could only result in the disappearance of the semi-
feudal state that everywhere had accompanied the
beginnings of industry. The latter emerged from the
primitive individualism under which it had originated, ready to be unified into great corporations
whose status in the community was still undefined.
A McKinley, and in fact most Presidents who in the
past had risen to power imbued with narrower ideas
of their duties, would have continued to remain
passive before the strides then taken by big business.
One may magnify the unrest which prevailed as the
result of the transformation taking place, and exaggerate the danger of social revolution, although
the New York 'World' expressed the opinion that the
United States was never so near to one as when
Roosevelt became President. Without the action
which he initiated, the dissatisfaction occasioned by
the trusts would have been driven underground to
work in a more dangerous manner. Roosevelt's real
achievement was inherently conservative, however
radical it then seemed to many. Underneath the
occasional extravagance of his language and the
violence of his denunciation, he upheld the best
interests of capital through hacking off top-heavy
bulges in its structure in order to leave it on a more
secure foundation.

The individualist in Roosevelt dimly perceived that the vast accumulations of capital, even when controlled by a single brain, were actually almost anonymous expressions of economic forces rolled together by one hand. The struggle of the trusts for growth was not unlike the action of organisms under a microscope when instinctively these seek accretion. On the surface such forces appeared to obey a master will. But the master, although he might cherish the illusion of possession, was more often a slave and at most only the pilot of an hour.

Roosevelt was least of all disturbed by the economic aspects of the trusts. He studied their effects with assiduous industry and refused to be stampeded into hasty action. Primarily he was no economist, and all his life, questions of this nature occupied him mainly when he could not escape from them. The trusts as instruments of production he regarded as necessary and even desirable steps in the evolution of our industrial life. To explain his varied attitude toward these and relieve it from the charge of inconsistency, he put forward a theory, in carefully balanced words, that trusts were both good and bad, and his attacks on corporations would be succeeded by statements praising their merits.

Other aspects in the development of trusts he condemned. Power centered in the hands of a few individuals able to regulate at will the transportation of the country became dangerous to the community at large. When corporations used the great means at their disposal to attempt to influence public opinion, legislation, and courts, to build up a mastery over the vast resources of the United States and a monopoly of its thoroughfares, it became time for the Government acting in the people's interest to assert a right of supervision and control. The theory of Hamilton that the State must be omnipotent and could brook no rival fitted all the more readily with Roosevelt's ideas, because he himself was President. The struggle which then took place was between a statesman who, in the presence of unfamiliar expressions of financial control, was endeavoring to shape the powers of Government in order to retain its supremacy, and new business methods which were then in the process of rapid development and the lasting significance of which was to be looked for in the economic order they were creating, often by harsh methods. The opposition between the State and the trusts was not irreconcilable and the problem was one of adjustment more than of victory for either.

After the political came the human side of Roosevelt's attitude. The lesser importance attached to other distinctions than wealth in America, particularly around the turn of the century, had led to an exaggerated respect for money as the badge of success. The millionaire class became almost a recognized institution with riches regarded as a fitting accompaniment to virtue. Roosevelt did much to demolish the crude vulgarity of this belief. Terms he then coined, like 'malefactors of great wealth,' passed into the ordinary currency of speech. He helped to form a public opinion which shook big business from its assumption of inherent merit and forced the revision of its methods. With increased emphasis he was repeating from the White House the same opinions about corrupt wealth which twenty years before he had proclaimed in the Assembly at Albany. Perhaps he was the only public man of prominence in America who had never felt that respect was due to riches for their own sake.

Roosevelt despised many millionaires as *parvenus* risen like beanstalks, who had nothing to recommend them save their money. Most of these, he thought, were without capacity for enjoying the real sense of life or the appreciation of all that ennobled its expression. He preferred Western desperadoes, who at least ran physical risks, to the hard-faced and soft-bodied Wall Street financiers. Riches at no time had been his goal. Public life, letters, and sport always seemed so much worthier pursuits. He had never been really affluent and at times had been obliged to struggle with straitened means. It was distasteful for him to see the exaggerated rewards lavished on those who only pursued wealth, and to find respect for money out of all proportion to the services rendered the community. He challenged these services and intended to show up the illegality of certain of the rich. Modernized under a democratic garb, there was something of the feudal lord in Roosevelt, in the loyalties he inspired, in his sense of personal mastery, and even in his instinctive prejudices. He could find a dozen excellent reasons for denouncing some Wall Street magnate, but deep down, perhaps the truest was his unexpressed aversion for a type of life and a goal repugnant to his nature.

His hostility ran deeper than if this had come only

from the antagonism provoked by opposite concep-
tions of business ethics. The defense of popular
rights acted as a powerful incentive to the politician
in him. Roosevelt was no demagogue at heart, though
to shallow observers at times he appeared one. But
he knew that the attacks leveled against him in Wall
Street endeared him to the mass of the people. They
made for his popularity among tens of millions of
small Americans who kept faith in him as their
leader.

The President threw himself impetuously into the
struggle. He attacked the corporations for their
attempts to influence legislation and the judiciary,
and then did the same himself in order to restrain the
corporations. He held the whip of patronage over
Congress to force support for his measures. The
politician and the fighter made him utilize every
means he could, proper or questionable, in order to
gain his way. It was said that he was popular in
Congress because he didn't care a damn for the law.
As in the Panama affair, the goal was all-important,
the method indifferent. He was ready to use personal
influence, cajolery, or threat. In one great case he
did not hesitate to remind the magistrate of a high
court that he expected from him a favorable decision.

The reference to the trusts in his first Message to
Congress had been mild and measured, weighted
with phrases kept in strict balance. The announce-
ment of the Government's intention to test the
validity of the Northern Securities merger came as a
masterpiece of restrained statement. No one was ever

less of a 'country lawyer,' as Wall Street soon discovered, than Attorney-General Knox, who instituted
this suit. He had been reared at Pittsburgh in an
atmosphere of newly formed corporations and knew
where to pierce their weakness. His incisive mind,
brilliant though spasmodic in its activity, was then
of enormous assistance to the President.

Consternation was aroused by the Government's
action. J. P. Morgan hurried to Washington, and
Roosevelt's own account of their meeting is a chapter
of pure comedy which no one enjoyed more keenly
than the President. If its humor appealed to him,
he also relished the occasion of asserting the Government's authority by sousing the bankers with correc-
titudes about enforcing the law in Wall Street. Morgan's personal comments are unrecorded save by
Roosevelt, but James J. Hill, who was equally concerned with Morgan, delivered himself of a chagrined
statement. Opinions are usually formed in youth and
Hill's impression of Federal officials originated
probably with a few Government appointees of
doubtful standing he had known in his early days
out West. He felt genuinely grieved at the injustice
of being compelled to fight 'against the political
adventurers who have never done anything but pose
and draw their salaries.' Both Morgan and Hill
according to their lights were high-minded and
patriotic citizens and few men have done better work
as empire builders than Hill. But both regarded
Roosevelt's action to dissolve the Northern Securities
merger in the nature of a personal offense deliberately
undertaken by a politician swayed by questionable

motives, with a view to their injury. For honest men
to assume this attitude justifies Roosevelt's action in
preventing the railroads of the country from becoming one great unrestrained monopoly.

The President was no enemy of capital, though he
was of many capitalists. Of others he remained a
close friend. Bacon and Perkins, who were among his
intimates, both came out of Morgan's office. Paul
Morton had grown up in the railway business. Root,
the foremost corporation lawyer of his day, called
Roosevelt in a public speech 'the great conservator
of property and of rights.' The President, rarely
original in his ideas, and always so in his methods,
followed a middle course and took the view that the
solution of the abuses lay not in crushing the trusts,
but in devising means of supervision and control.
It was another way of applying the authority of the
State to meet unforeseen developments. The measures he advocated, like the power to fix rates, which
now appears elementary, awakened at the time a
storm of indignant disapproval. Great financiers
denounced the President as an anarchist and a madman, while he affirmed with reason that he was the
best friend of property. Many then entertained
serious doubts as to his sanity and scurrilous stories,
not confined to whispers, went the rounds about him.
The only effect of these attacks was to arouse his
fighting instincts. The old pugnacity was reawakened.
He knew he was being outrageously misrepresented
and maligned by the people he disliked most, the
smugly rich and the Wall Street crowd with vast
means at their disposal to hire the best lawyers and

keep under their thumb the public press. Purely as a sporting proposition he enjoyed the fight.

IX

The night of his election in 1904, Roosevelt issued a famous statement:

'The wise custom which limits the President to two terms regards the substance and not the form, and under no circumstances will I be a candidate for or accept another nomination.'

Some of Roosevelt's closest friends have expressed as their opinion to the writer that he paid little attention to this statement until, during the winter of 1907–08, he made up his mind not to be a candidate again. This is quite possible, for it was never Roosevelt's practice to ruminate or retract a decision, but it only confirms the inherent sincerity of his original declaration by proving that even after an interval of several years his mind reacted identically on being confronted by the same situation. When Roosevelt later was approaching the end of his term as President, it was said that he would have given his right hand not to have made this pronouncement. He may have bitterly regretted his words, for they barred every decent possibility for the continuation of his own power in the White House. But the poignancy of his regret confirmed the reasons which stood behind this statement. Roosevelt, seemingly most impulsive of men, rarely said anything on impulse, and the renunciation of his future power as President came from a hidden deliberate thought, long matured in solitude, and which awaited appro-

priate occasion for its delivery. It was the result of
a deep struggle within himself and proceeded from
the wells of patriotism and duty which guided him in
solemn moments.

Rightly he believed that his place in history would
show him in a more disinterested light by his renunciation than if he attempted to violate a tradition
handed down from the Nation's birth. With his
instinct for the workings of the popular mind, he
knew that many people would feel disappointed if
he tried to occupy the Presidency longer than Washington had held it. 'Some,' as he shrewdly wrote,
'until I consented to run might think that they
wished me to run.' He treasured his place in history
far too deeply to risk destroying this confidence.
Our first President's example influenced his decision,
for he tried to shape his conduct, whenever similarity
was possible, on that of Washington and Lincoln.
But it was more than this. The patriotic statesman
in him understood the temptation to which the
ambitious politician would afterward be exposed.
Before it was too late, he intended to block his own
path by the only barriers which could deter him.
He knew his character too well not to realize that
taunts, attacks, or opposition would merely sharpen
his zest to tempt him to overcome his own restraints.
It was necessary to place a firm inhibition on record
at once, in final opposition to the secret hopes he
still might cherish. Nothing has ever been more to
the credit of Roosevelt than this pronouncement
made at the moment of his highest triumph. When
later some chance utterances or thoughts half spoken

left on their hearers the impression of a bitter regret, this only proved the deliberate purpose which stood behind his original statement.

Political hairsplitting provides an American form for intellectual speculation which in another age found ingenious occupation in trying to solve theological problems. The intentions of Presidents who do not choose to run again replace the sex of angels as appropriate subjects for discussion over the ambiguities hidden under words. The country at large rightly saw in Roosevelt's statement an election pledge that he would not again seek the nomination. But many still remained skeptical, for there was a general feeling among politicians that he might accept the candidacy if this was thrust upon him. Even Lodge wrote him [14] that in the end he might be forced, 'in order to save not your policies and the party but your friends.' Others, too, began to qualify his statement by reading into it new meanings about future eventual intentions. They did not realize that the greatest value it possessed was the pledge Theodore Roosevelt had made to himself, and to which every honorable consideration obliged him to conform. Henceforth, whatever occurred, Roosevelt was the only American who could not aspire to become a candidate in 1908. Deliberately he had raised himself to a height from which there could be no honorable descent.

Roosevelt the statesman had by his initiative compelled his own departure from the White House, but Roosevelt the politician had no intention of allowing any avoidable diminution of his future per-

sonal influence over party affairs. He may have felt
that this was fair compensation for what later he
called his *quixotism* and that he possessed the moral
right to expect a successor, whom he would help to
elect, to continue his famous policies. Firmly persuaded, not without cause, that he had been the
regenerator of the Republican Party, rightly proud of
his Administration and of the confidence reposed in
him by the American people, it seemed natural that
part of the price for his self-denial should be paid by
expecting the continuation of the measures he had
advocated and which appeared to him of vital importance for the country. This was hardly put into
words, for the gentleman in Roosevelt was incapable
of expressing a bargain framed on his own disinterestedness. But only by an assumption of this nature
is it possible to explain Roosevelt's later attitude
toward Taft.

Undoubtedly, he derived keen enjoyment from his
ability to transmit the prophet's mantle. Lesser
considerations did not disturb him, and he could
play the politician to his heart's content, without a
qualm of conscience.

The interior organization of a party hardly concerns the general public. The average American
labors under the delusion that he maintains interest
in politics because every four years he can be lashed
into a temporary enthusiasm which may last for a
few weeks. After he has tried to elect some candidate
submitted to his approval by a series of processes
very remote from his control, he resumes ordinary
occupations, indifferent to what occurs unless his

particular interests are visibly touched. Politics, like baseball, is a sport mainly for the professional. The silent organization of a party, peg by peg, offers nothing spectacular and little that is interesting to the layman. How often do delegates elected at the primaries who control the nominations, interest the average voter?

As President, Roosevelt had relished the opportunity to fill the Republican organization with men of his own confidence. It was a slow, patient labor, based largely on petty patronage, and which had to be carried out carefully so as to avoid violent disruptions. Roosevelt had been used to this kind of work ever since he had run as a candidate for the New York Assembly. Instead of fighting the machine, he now was an essential part of the machine, and except for certain limitations, which he understood to a hairbreadth, he felt able to do pretty much as he wished. These limitations he afterward described as his inability at the 1908 Convention to nominate either an extreme progressive or an extreme conservative.

The real feeling of the Old Guard in Congress who disliked him was to prevent the nomination from going to Roosevelt and secure a successor whom he could not control. Speaker Cannon, Senator Knox, Secretary Shaw, even Vice-President Fairbanks, were all mentioned and dropped as likely candidates. Roosevelt's own thoughts traveled first to Root. He felt for him a warm personal friendship which, even after the break in 1912, saved Root from many a shaft. The President admired the lucid intelligence which enabled the latter, at the same time that he analyzed a situation, to discern the remedy. Root, shrewdest and most loyal of counselors, had not as yet been shrewd enough, for his own ambition, to allay the suspicion which the West then entertained for him. The association of his legal career with the great moneyed interests in Wall Street still remained a background to disqualify him as a candidate. Roosevelt, generously appreciative of Root's merit as a statesman, was never easily influenced by motives of friendship to err over a political endorsement of the wrong horse. He would gladly, so he declared, crawl on hands and knees from the White House to the Capitol, if he could bring about Root's nomination, but the Westerners would never stand for him. Bryan was certain to make an anti-trust campaign and Root's reputation as a great corporation lawyer would endanger the election.

Our democracy becomes immensely more appreciative of talent when it realizes that nothing is asked of it. The reputations of Root and also of Hughes have risen steadily to their present great height as soon as it became apparent that neither any longer desired the Presidency nor coveted popular favor to obtain office. But Root as a possible candidate had not then attained the eminence of great public service with the reputation of disinterestedness which was later to be his reward. And better than any one in the country Roosevelt was then in a position to gauge public opinion.

Toward Hughes the situation was different. His spectacular elevation to the New York Governorship, the admiration felt for his character and ability, the trust reposed in him by the people, all pointed to the promise of a great future career which has since been attained, though not in the sense that then seemed probable. Roosevelt began by professing to share in the general admiration. Although there was little personal sympathy between them, for a time he appeared to regard Hughes with favor in the light of a possible successor. What reasons suddenly made him withhold his approval? The secret is locked in Roosevelt's heart, but the knowledge of certain circumstances permits a surmise to be made.

When later Roosevelt discussed his relations with Taft, he insisted that personal feelings had nothing to do with his public course and that he was selected solely as being the best candidate. This may be true, though perhaps not only for the reasons he gave. He stated that by a turn of the hand he could have 'thrown the nomination to either Taft or Hughes.' [15] If personal friendship had nothing to do with his choice, why did he prefer the former?

Although Roosevelt had rejected the Presidential nomination in 1908, he was extremely anxious for Republican success. He felt with some reason that the austerity in Hughes's character and his remoteness from the politician's world of reality might not make him the best candidate. Hughes, at that time indifferent to political arts, had not yet become known for the courteous charm of manner which was to distinguish him.

Possibly secret reasons also existed in Roosevelt's heart against the choice of Hughes. The day he ceased to be President, he would be deprived of many of the means then at his command. Was it to his interest to see a successor in the White House from his native city, who had repeated his own performance as a reforming Governor of New York, whose intellectual powers and ability he had every reason to respect, and who was likely to remain a rival as long as he lived? Was it to his ultimate interest that later there should be two ex-Presidents from New York, both with strong personalities, both with a large following, and who could not always be expected to see eye to eye?

He would hardly have been human if thoughts of this nature did not traverse his mind, even though unformulated, possibly to remain without influence on his decision. An incident occurred, however, which came as a watershed in Roosevelt's relations to Hughes. The latter as Governor had been hard-pressed by the Republican organization in New York to appoint as Superintendent of Elections a man whom he regarded as an improper selection for the office. Roosevelt in his 'Autobiography' has described in detail a similar incident at a time when he, then Governor of New York, had also been urged by the machine to make an improper appointment and his refusal to do so, in spite of the pressure which then threatened him with political extinction. In this case Hughes was equally determined, although like Roosevelt he also offered to name another organization man. A personal message was then conveyed to Governor Hughes, which came from the White House. Roosevelt sent word that, although he did not wish to interfere in the internal affairs of New York, he would be glad if Hughes could appoint the candidate recommended by the organization. The Governor's answer the same day was to transmit the name of another man, but from that time Roosevelt's relations with him were no longer the same.

The country was then waiting to know whether Hughes would be the candidate. A committee of the New York Republican Club proposed a meeting which would give the Governor the opportunity to speak on national issues. He agreed to this and the staging had been arranged in order to open the campaign. The President was unable to attend, although he knew that the Governor would that night make an important speech. By a strange coincidence, Roosevelt had ready an unexpected Message for delivery to Congress, which was sent in too late for the evening papers and had to appear next morning when Hughes's address to the New York Republican Club would also be reported. This Message, which dealt with 'malefactors of great wealth,' was sensational enough to cover the front page of every newspaper in the country, to be discussed for days. The publicity of Governor Hughes's carefully prepared speech was lost. It had to be cut down, forced into a corner, and forgotten amid the controversies aroused by the President's arguments.

At a time when the choice for the nomination still appeared to lie between Taft and Root, a popular squib ran

'Taft and the world Taft's with you,
Root and you Root alone.'

There was a pleasing geniality about Taft which made for his wide popularity. He possessed many warm friends and no personal enemies. His career as an administrator had been distinguished, his legal training sound, and his figure presented no angularities which made for friction. Roosevelt, who had already offered him a seat on the Supreme Court Bench, was warmly attached to him as a friend, and doubtless felt that the absence of masterfulness in his character and the impression he gave of reluctance to impose his will, which did not seem shaped in any very original direction, made him the more available candidate. He also had proved himself an admirable lieutenant, which helped to point him to Roosevelt as a natural successor. Another unmentioned reason — he came from Ohio, not New York.

There is room for different opinions as to what the attitude of a President in the White House should be when toward the end of his second term the Convention of his party meets to nominate a candidate. Does partisanship or does neutrality offer the proper course? Roosevelt's partisanship for Taft had an excellent excuse. 'The only way,' he wrote, 'to prevent my own nomination was for me actively to champion and to force through the nomination of some one else; I chose Taft rather than Hughes, and I still think I was wise.'

Roosevelt knew how easily he could have had the 1908 nomination for himself, and there was truth in his statement that he worked harder to prevent this than most Presidential candidates to capture it. When his most intimate friend Senator Lodge addressed the Convention as Chairman after praising Roosevelt's renunciation, it was to say that any one who attempted to use his name as a candidate impugned his sincerity and good faith. The rest is history. Roosevelt had succeeded in nominating his successor and the American people confirmed his choice.

CHAPTER III

ADVERSITY

I

AFTER Lycurgus had induced the Spartans to accept his reforms, he obtained their promise to abide by them until his return from distant travels. Some say that purposely he never came back. Different versions of this legend exist, and there are as many different versions about Roosevelt's later intentions when he left the White House for Africa at the end of his second term.

What ought an ex-President to do? No American, without a sense of shame, can read about General Grant writing against an impending painful death in order to leave a pittance to his family. With Roosevelt this problem did not arise, and he professed to find something attractive in a President leaving office to return to private life ready to take up any honorable work. On the eve of his departure from the White House, he wrote a letter to the Kaiser to say that it was most unlikely he would ever hold office again, but that if war should come while he still enjoyed bodily vigor, he would endeavor to secure permission to raise a division of mounted rifles.

Roosevelt stepped from the Presidency with a halo all his own. The unshaped ambitions of his youth had been gratified beyond his wildest expectations. Having written his name large in the country's history, he could not do greater things, and he knew the risk of undertaking anything which might cause him to sink in the public esteem. He was still young, in rugged health, and brimming over with forceful vitality. For ten years, seven of which had been spent in the White House, he filled not only the Presidency, but the foremost place in American life. He had shaped, led, aroused to enthusiasm, and infuriated different wings of opinion. But never had he failed to interest the country.

He knew that his presence in the United States at the beginning of a new administration for which he was so largely responsible would be unfair to his successor. It was necessary to go far away in order to avoid the semblance of influence over Taft. Motives of a different order suggested the course he should take. The friend, even the politician, counseled distance from the capital, and the unexpressed artist's instinct in his nature understood that second to occupying the stage, which circumstances then made impossible, the next best thing was to disappear completely for the time. His early taste as a hunter was responsible for the first step of his new activity. One treasures the recollections of youth and, remembering his experiences after big game in the Rockies twenty-five years earlier, he thought that Africa would offer the chance for something of a great adventure.

While the Republican Convention nominated his successor, Roosevelt was already developing the plan for his African journey. Big-game shooting no longer satisfied his sense of what was fitting. He wished his itinerary to take a scientific aspect rather than one only for sport and pleasure. Boyhood delights as a naturalist could be revived. The chase was to be after specimens intended for the National Museum at Washington, which would send with him field naturalists and taxidermists to skin and cure the game he would shoot.

The journey offered also a financial inducement. He wanted to make money, though only in a manner which he could reconcile with ideas of propriety. His former publisher proposed fifty thousand dollars for the serial rights of the African narrative. Another firm had offered twice as much, but acceptance of the first seemed more dignified. 'There is such a thing as making too much money out of a given feat,' he wrote to Lodge.[1] Under no circumstances was he willing to make a commercial use of his name. The gentleman spoke in Roosevelt, for no one was ever more indifferent about money. George Washington had once alluded to his own distaste for what he called 'ostentatious disinterestedness.' Roosevelt also felt some disquiet at appearing quixotic. But the quixotism back in his mind was not primarily over money matters, though he referred to these, but because of the rejected third term which always wormed its way into his thought.

Before leaving America, Roosevelt had arranged to become an editorial writer with 'The Outlook,' after refusing higher offers from other periodicals. Lyman Abbott, the editor, was a personal friend, and by his association with a paper of its character he intended to provide a suitable mouthpiece for the expression of his opinions on his return to the United States.

At the Gridiron Club dinner shortly before he sailed, Roosevelt jokingly remarked that 'Wall Street expects every lion to do his duty.' But from the time he was out of bounds, so to speak, criticism vanished. His life in Africa was mainly interesting for reasons other than sport. The nine lions which fell to his gun were of as little consequence in his life as the fact that the natives then called him 'the man with the large paunch,' euphemistically translated for his benefit as 'the man with unerring aim'! More significant is the picture of Roosevelt at work in his tent after the day's chase, dictating articles and preparing the lectures he had been invited to deliver. In the relaxing atmosphere of the tropics his energy never flagged. As a pastime he read serious books, and for the first time in his life enjoyed Shakespeare. Even in the jungle he found occasion to expatiate on the merits of Macaulay, whose hammer-like style and delight in the loudly shouted obvious appealed to his own sermonizing taste. Habits of assiduous application long ingrained made him utilize a holiday as an enjoyable toil. After seven years' intense strain in the White House, his journey to Africa provided occasion for more work than play.

Roosevelt might lure himself into the belief that his only concern was how to shoot rhino and lions. This self-deception did not last, for his combativeness against wild animals no longer satisfied him. He felt haunting doubts as to whether it would again be possible for him to do anything more. The moral solitude of his African journey encouraged speculation of this kind. He had lost touch with men and events at

home and felt depressed, though, unwilling to admit
this to himself, he professed to enjoy every moment of
his time. Hunting, writing, traveling would have
occupied fully any ordinary mortal. But behind him
stood the record of a great achievement with the
lurking regret of a lost opportunity, and before him
loomed the question mark of his future. He wrote to
Lodge [2] that he hadn't a thought about politics and
in the next sentence disapproved of Taft's removal
from office of men he had appointed. Already from
East Africa he insisted that he would not make any
prediction about what he proposed later to do or discuss with any one whether he would return to political
life. His thoughts wandered from one conjecture to
another. Sometimes he saw his future in the Senate,
and at others he saw no future at all, 'for people
easily grow tired of the advice of a man whose day is
past.' [3] Then, as later, while his better judgment
counseled him to seek detachment from political
strife, the restless blood in his veins found repose in
the prospect of struggle.

A letter from Lodge [4] reached him in the Sudan,
warning him about the situation in Washington.
There is usually an obvious common-sense in the
shrewdest politician's advice, and Lodge urged
Roosevelt to say nothing about American politics to
any newspaper man until his return home. He also
advised him not to remain in exile for another year
as some then urged him to do, nor to hurry back without carrying out his original intention of passing
through Europe.

'There is a constantly growing thought of you and

your return to the Presidency,' wrote Lodge, with
more than a hint about the workings of his own mind.
He reminded Roosevelt that the American people
were looking to him for leadership. But Lodge, always a regular, could only conceive of Roosevelt in
the line of a regular succession as the organization
candidate. Even then he feared lest his name might
be connected with quarrels within the Administration.
He must remain aloof from all such bickerings and
save his future from criticism. Sounder advice was
never given him, for already every one discontented
with the Taft Administration was looking to Roosevelt for help. Pinchot, removed from office by Taft,
journeyed abroad to meet him. Newspaper men,
some utterly hostile to the new Administration, were
waiting at Khartum, hoping to extract some word
from him to which they could attach their animosity.
Roosevelt emerged from the jungle only to find himself again acclaimed as the leader.

For a moment the center of American political
interest lay in the Sudan. Then an interlude of
months occurred during which Roosevelt trium-
phantly progressed through the capitals of Europe.
When still in America he had expressed some reluctance to exploit his position as a former President
by any grand tour. Pride and an inherent good taste
made him a little unwilling to appear to solicit receiving the attentions of royalty. Often in the past
he had spoken scornfully of those Americans who
sought presentation at Court and expressed satisfaction in the fact that he and Mrs. Roosevelt had refused
this for themselves, years before. It was a bit distasteful to seem to go back on this attitude.

He was frankly pleased to be invited to give the Romanes Lecture at Oxford and to speak in the Sorbonne. Deep down he tried to feel as if his real profession in life had been that of an historian, and political activities were rather in the nature of temporary occupations, certain of which he had tried to prolong. Historical writing provided him with a justification for existence beyond the hazards of politics.

The shower of academic honors seemed tributes to his merit as a scholar, and the invitations from learned bodies were at once followed by invitations from royalty. He could not go to Oxford without seeing the King, but he now felt a reasonable excuse in his own mind for seeking a royal audience. He could not visit Paris without going to Berlin, or to Brussels without proceeding to The Hague. He could hardly pick and choose, and there was always an excellent reason for accepting. How was it possible otherwise? Once the first wall of reluctance, raised more by pride than by taste, had broken down, he could not refuse, and there was much to tempt him. Never before had such honors been extended to an ex-President; never before had an American been invited to become the guest of kings. Frankly, he enjoyed the novel experience and forgot all his former inhibitions.

Certain incidents occurred which gave him a not unwelcome occasion to assert himself. An ill-advised attempt by the Vatican to extract from him a secret pledge not to visit the Methodist Mission in Rome, after a proposed audience with the Pope, was straightway rejected. Tactiessly, certain Methodists then attempted to exploit this refusal, which Roosevelt countered by publicly canceling his arrangements to meet them. He might profess to believe that by his independence he had injured his future political prospects in giving offense to two of the most powerful creeds in America, but deep down he knew better. An affront to either might have been detrimental, but his old method of balancing opposites now stood him in good stead, and by asserting his independence of both he alienated neither. Again, when the Kaiser overlooked Mrs. Roosevelt in his invitation to the former President to be his guest in Berlin, Roosevelt's declination of the invitation brought a prompt amend from the Emperor.

His impressions of royalty have been chronicled in a lengthy narrative, written down at Sir George Trevelyan's request, but really intended for posterity, and perhaps because of this lacking in some of his customary humor. His observations, though full of good sense, are deficient in incisive penetration. They are written from the point of view of a man who, professedly a democrat, saw kings from a pedestal at least as lofty as their own; who was neither impressed nor hostile, and who sincerely appreciated their virtues and conscientious sense of duty. The proximity of royalty left Roosevelt with no sense of envy, for in his own experience he had gone far beyond their feeling of power. The kings he met seemed to him almost objects of commiseration whose exalted position raised a barrier to prevent comradeship with the men who really did the things that count. He could not imagine a more appallingly dreary life for any man of ambition.[5]

Yet he enjoyed his experiences intensely. There had always been a sociable quality in Roosevelt which made him take interest in people of every description high or low, and it was agreeable to find that recognition of his merit came whole-heartedly from both extremes. His travels in Europe made him feel as if he stood on the same plane as monarchs, and he wrote Lodge that he was treated as if he combined the functions of a visiting sovereign with other attributes. Kings asked him to sit on their right hand in the carriage, 'as almost all the kings did — I suppose on the theory that I was a kind of ex-sovereign myself.[6] He did not realize that this was only because they regarded him as their guest. They treated him, he wrote, with intimacy and on a footing of equality, and in turn he liked 'almost all the various kings and queens I met.'

His professed attitude was that of a private citizen with no claim to precedence, and content to walk, sit, or stand anywhere or below any one. This attitude admittedly was assumed less in a spirit of humility than of pride. Deep down he knew he was Roosevelt, who felt no need for pretending that he was an imitation king. He knew the honors that were his due, that his seeming modesty would never be admitted, and that wherever he went he would find himself the guest of the day.

Most of all he enjoyed his stay at Budapest. The Magyar aristocracy, with their strong sense of leadership, their alleged liberalism, and their fondness for big-game shooting, were also men of the world. In their lives he saw something after the pattern of his own. He appreciated the charm of their manner, and the cheer of their hospitality, even when he omitted to inquire into the feudal condition of their peasantry. In London and in Paris, where he stood on more familiar ground, he felt that it was not necessary to observe all the reticences he had imposed on himself in stranger capitals. He was genuinely fond of the English and the French, and he saw before him an opportunity to speak to them as a candid friend. He had preached so long to Americans that it was also pleasant to be able to tell foreign nations tactfully how to handle their problems. In the Sorbonne address, amid the approval of moralists, he expatiated on the dangers of race suicide. At the Guildhall in London, he dwelt on the 'white man's burden' in Egypt, only to advise the English to rule with a strong hand or else to leave. The criticism by a few of the alleged inopportuneness of certain of his remarks was more than stifled amid the chorus of approval which these elicited. The straight talk to effete civilizations, cartooned by 'Punch' with its jest at the sermon-like quality of his utterances, was too occasional to leave any unfavorable remembrance.

It was all a wonderful epilogue to his career as a man as well as a President. Throughout the world there existed a vast reservoir of admiration for his character. The scholar and the sportsman, the soldier and the statesman, but above all the man in Roosevelt had touched deep chords of sympathy in different lands. He was then at the height of his fame which

THE WISDOM OF THE WEST

nothing had yet dimmed. And America thrilled with pride at the honors showered on the greatest of her living sons.

II

'The country is awaiting you anxiously — not out of mere curiosity to know what your attitude will be, but to lead it, to give it direction.... Your personal following is larger to-day than it has ever been,' wrote Franklin K. Lane, who was a Democrat, to Roosevelt, then in Europe.

The salvos of guns and the applause of millions greeted Roosevelt on his return to New York, June 18, 1910. He had been gone some fifteen months. No sovereign returning to his kingdom after an absence could have received a more enthusiastic welcome. From the time when his steamer was met in the harbor by a naval parade to the time when a great procession escorted him through the streets of his native city, his home-coming was one great triumph such as no American had ever before received. That afternoon Roosevelt was recognized going out of a bookstore on Fifth Avenue. A crowd at once gathered around to cheer him and shake his hand. Describing the incident to a member of his family later in the day, he remarked, 'It is a kind of hysteria. They will soon be throwing rotten eggs at me.'

In his reply to the Mayor's greeting at the landing, Roosevelt had declared that he was ready and eager to do his part to help solve the national problems. Already this speech had been interpreted to mean his return to active politics. So long as he stood on a pedestal the whole country was prepared to applaud. Many of his admirers and friends urged him to remain on this elevation of detachment. He knew that he had nothing to gain by plunging into politics and much to lose. But there was a craving within him beyond his control. When still in the White House, had he not avowed that the rôle of a sage held out no attractions for him?

Undoubtedly he tried to trace certain limitations to his future political activity. He insisted that he did not want office and suggestions conveyed to him that he might be disposed to accept the Mayoralty or the Governorship were promptly rejected. His brief experience when presiding over the Senate, and subsequent altercations with Senators, also left a distaste for the wrangling propensities of the Upper Chamber. In all sincerity he tried to persuade others and perhaps himself that he cherished no public ambition, would undertake no active political work, and wanted not even the Presidency.

A man of lesser energy might have succeeded in holding this line. Grover Cleveland could spend his declining years at Princeton respected by all, but Roosevelt found no slackening in his own vitality. He declared that before two months he would make no political statement, yet ten days after he had landed, against every inclination, and against his own better judgment, he was already engaged in a bitter factional fight in New York for the enactment of a direct primary law which Governor Hughes was then trying to put through and for which he had solicited his aid. It was impossible for Roosevelt to

throw himself into any fight at a safe distance or
without assuming leadership. His record, his supporters, his temperament, would never have tolerated
taking a secondary part in any contest. Twenty
years earlier he would have relished just such a fight,
but then he had everything to gain and the background of the Presidency did not soar behind him.
Now violating his better judgment, he found himself
forced to take sides against the machine in a partisan
issue which was only of small importance to him. If
the popular election of Senators has not brought a
redress for the evils it then was confidently expected
to cure, it seemed a movement in the right direction,
and the decent people who supported this measure,
and who had formerly supported him, required all
the help they could obtain in their fight. Roosevelt
the reformer, lifelong apostle of good citizenship,
could not hold aloof in his native State from a contest
over an issue in which he felt strong convictions,
merely because this seemed more expedient. What
were all his professions worth if he did not enter the
fray on behalf of his friends at the time when his
services were most needed?

He was overwhelmed with requests from all over
the country. Two thousand invitations came in two
months, to visit, to speak, to help in different causes
and in different States. In August, he went West,
escorted by some twenty-odd correspondents, to
attend the Frontier Celebration at Cheyenne. It was
hardly the way to avoid political publicity, but he
justified his course, at least in his own eyes, by
proposing to make addresses only on non-political

subjects. These were all carefully prepared in accordance with his usual practice and distributed to the press for release as delivered. To the crowds who gathered everywhere to greet him, he also made a number of five-minute speeches from the rear platform of his train. The West had provided him with his youthful interest and his first popularity. On its wide expanse he found a welcome interlude of change from the over-moneyed East. He felt at home on the plains, and enjoyed the hearty enthusiasm of his reception. And he tried to persuade himself and others that he was helping Taft by helping the Republican Party in the West.

His relations with Taft, whom he had not been to see after his return from Europe, had since the election labored under a strain. It could hardly be otherwise. Formerly in the Orient when a prince rested under too deep obligations to a subject and no other reward seemed adequate, he usually caused the subject to be murdered. But Taft was no Sultan and lacked homicidal propensities. He had felt intense gratitude to Roosevelt and his nature was kindly, loyal, and warm-hearted. But he could not forget that he was President of the United States with all the responsibilities of the position and the necessity of justifying himself in his own esteem and that of his supporters. The power he took over from Roosevelt on March 4, 1909, then appeared a continuation, more than a succession, but every day that went by made greater the distance from its origin. New circumstances had arisen, new men had appeared, and altered conditions added to the perplexities of the

situation. Taft found himself confronted by unexpected difficulties which required political art to
compose, and no one was ever less of a politician.
The most peaceful of men was plunged into bitter
quarrels against every inclination. The jurist in his
early training spoke inwardly to affirm the principles
of law which made him hark back to the conservatism
of legality. While this took place, Roosevelt more
and more, as if the better to bring out the contrast
with Taft, felt that his own deepest convictions lay
on the side of the President's adversaries. He drama-
tized the life of the country as one vast struggle
between opposing forces of reaction and progress,
property and humanity, good and evil, and persuaded
himself that it was his mission to make the fight for
righteousness.

The West was seething with fierce discussions over
the questions of Referendum, Initiative, and Recall, a
trinity of reforms which many then felt convinced
would bring about the salvation of pure democracy
after its long years of suffering in a corrupted political
atmosphere. The desire for some fresh principle,
proclaimed by its believers as a remedy certain to
confer untold benefits on the nation which adopts it
is characteristic of the mass appeal always receptive
to an easy formula. Particularly is this true in a new
country, in which abuses are often more glaring and
respect for tradition less deep-seated than in long-
settled and more skeptical communities. It was
always characteristic of Roosevelt to welcome novelty
for its own sake, perhaps because instinctively he felt
that some of his ability to interest the people came

from his power to adapt himself to fresh circumstances and make these his own. In the rising tide of his opposition to Taft, it was natural to attach himself to whatever would most pointedly mark the difference between his opinions and those of the President. Lastly, he espoused these reforms all the more enthusiastically because their origin lay in his beloved West.

Before the Colorado Legislature on August 29, 1910, he criticized the action of the United States Supreme Court when it declared unconstitutional a law designed to abolish unhealthy conditions in the bakeshops. His criticism was moderate in its tone and he cited the dissenting opinions of three Justices of the Supreme Court and quoted the words of Lincoln when the latter had said, in disapproval of the Dred Scott Decision, 'I believe the decision was improperly made and I go for reversing it.' Two days later, he made a speech at Ossawatomie, in Kansas, in which, with some oratorical flourish, he maintained that property should be the servant and not the master of the Commonwealth, and that the citizens of the United States must effectively control the mighty commercial forces which they themselves had called into being. Such phrases were really vague commonplaces which contained nothing very startling, and Roosevelt insisted then as before that he was the true friend of property. But a state of mind had grown up around him which owed its origin to the days in the Albany Legislature when he had first attacked corrupt wealth. Time and again he had infuriated men who found themselves threatened by his invective, and

time and again the hostility he awakened only subsided when Roosevelt no longer found occasion to
renew these attacks. As President, respect for the
office kept criticism within bounds or restricted this
to mutterings the rumblings of which even then filled
the public ear. But he was no longer President, and
already fast maneuvering himself into an opposition
to Taft which was more than suspected and must soon
break out publicly. His enemies saw no further
reason to observe the same restraints as before.
Savage attacks based on his speeches then treated
Roosevelt as a revolutionary and an incendiary. He
was accused of 'attacking the courts' and a vast
amount of virtuous indignation was aroused by many
who gratified their long-pent hatred of the man by a
dishonest misrepresentation of his argument.

Roosevelt had gone over his general attitude about
the courts with Justice Moody, of the United States
Supreme Court, who had drawn his attention to the
very decisions he referred to in his speech. Seemingly
impulsive, he had then acted on suggestions advanced
by lawyers in order to express ideas which were not
his own, but with which he sympathized. There was
nothing revolutionary in his position and there never
was anything revolutionary about Roosevelt. No
reformer has ever been so conservative. No one was
ever more careful to observe the conventional practices of life or held a more conventional outlook over
matters of general conduct. No fallacy has ever been
greater than the idea of Roosevelt as a revolutionary,
intent on subverting the institutions of the country.
But some of that spirit of veneration which in mon-

archical lands was formerly lavished on the reigning
dynasty has in America been conferred on the courts.
A halo peculiarly their own invests these and the form
of Roosevelt's pronouncement allowed for a certain
misunderstanding. His speech had in part been
impromptu and in part carefully prepared. Only the
latter portion, which was typewritten and had been
handed to the correspondents was given publicity.
The beginning and end of the address explaining his
meaning was omitted from the press accounts. In
quoting his speech certain sentences, designedly or
otherwise, were twisted out of their proper connection
until they helped to swell the general impression of his
radicalism.

Within three months of his return from Europe
greeted as a national hero, he had already aroused
the opposition of every conservative by his speeches
in the West, and reawakened that of every machine
politician in his native State by taking part in the
faction fight in New York.

It is bad enough to be obliged to make a fight when
there is a good chance of victory, but in this case there
was none. Opinion in New York he found mainly
lukewarm and even hostile to primary legislation.
Before him lay only a choice of evils, between certain
defeat and likely defeat.

In the 1910 election, the Republicans in New York
State, as Roosevelt had prophesied, were badly
beaten. Although he took credit for the fact that
without his intervention the Democratic majority
would have been still greater, Roosevelt found
that the feeling against him in New York, carefully

nursed by the machine, had become very bitter, and his enemies could now point out that under his lead the party had been badly thrashed. The only bright spot he professed to see was that it would put a stop to the talk of his nomination in 1912. His reason and his political sagacity kept proving to him the error of his future candidacy, while all along secret longings within were holding out its possibility before him.

III

Roosevelt had barely started on his Western trip in the summer of 1910 when a newspaper man who was in his confidence asked him how he would like to go again to the White House. 'I don't care *that* for it,' he said, snapping his thumb and forefinger together. 'I've had all the work and all the fun and all the glory of it, and I wouldn't give *that* [repeating his gesture] for any more of it.... Another term could not add anything to what I have had there. Of course if there were a big job of work to be done which the people of the country wanted me to handle, that would be a different thing.' [7]

This statement offered to a journalist he trusted explains the reasons in Roosevelt's mind which induced him to overcome his own better judgment. He knew that even if another term could be obtained, it was more likely than not to detract from his record, and after power, his position in history was perhaps the reward he most prized. Yet with full knowledge of this danger, he advanced step by step toward the disaster of 1912. The first premonition came two years before. Roosevelt was aware that the election of 1910 would at once be used by his enemies to shout that he was dead. To a friend who asked him, why, knowing what would happen, he had gone into the campaign, he answered, 'Because I couldn't live with myself if I didn't.' [8] He advanced as his reason that he felt under obligation to the men who had helped him in the past and now asked for his support. But it was more than any obligation, more than any sympathy with the direct primary issue. Reasons of this nature may have justified him in his own mind, or been utilized as arguments for others, but even without these he would have discovered some other ground. As soon as it came to taking part in a fight for a cause which he could ennoble and lead, every other consideration was thrown to the winds.

On his return from Europe, Roosevelt had been approached by Taft supporters to give a blanket endorsement of the new Administration. As he took no interest in tariff matters, he praised the President's action over the Tariff Board, but was unwilling to do more. He would have disapproved of any successor, and justified himself with the belief that an expression of approval would be bitterly resented by many of his staunchest friends. With political wisdom he still remained content to take a midway position and reserve his future course.

This position was one of extreme difficulty. In spite of professed disappointment with Taft, he had been ready to help the President's sympathizers in New York, at the same time that he advocated measures out West which he knew were distasteful to the Administration. He wrote Root [9] to say that very possibly he would even support Taft for the Presidency in the next election. Roosevelt had fallen foul of the insurgents and at first hardly realized himself where he stood. But a man with his temperament could not long continue floundering and undecided. Granting that it was impossible for him to remain detached, neutral, and aloof, what was there left to do? Whole-heartedly to support Taft was out of question and anything short of this would have been resented by the regulars. The private causes at the bottom of his first estrangement had been stifled only to come up again reënforced on the new grounds of public policy he had found. Not merely the man in Roosevelt felt deeply hurt in his feelings; it was also the politician and the statesman who had now persuaded himself that he could not compromise over questions which seemed rock-bottom principles. Taft, with the best intentions, had already driven a wedge into the heart of the Republican Party, and as the breach grew greater, he inclined always more toward the conservative wing. Perhaps unconsciously to emphasize his position, Roosevelt came to take a more radical attitude than the one he had hitherto assumed. So long as he was President, his policy had always been to steer a middle course in which he shouted directions loudly and startled the country more by his noise than by his innovations. The insurgents' undisciplined attitude and crude beliefs had been supremely distasteful to his instincts of sane leadership. Yet little by little the evolution of his attitude toward Taft caused him in all sincerity to espouse principles like the recall, which he had never before considered, which under other circumstances he might himself have denounced, and which later he dropped completely.

In analyzing the motives of a public man, it is impossible to weigh with any accuracy the variety of causes which lead him forward. Certain threads in Roosevelt's conduct at this time ran back, amid many interruptions, to the beginning of his political career. He could point to early origins in his sympathy for social justice and make a spirited defense of consistency for all he then upheld. Although persuading himself of his righteousness, his convictions were based more on the particularities of his position at this time than on sympathies expressed thirty years earlier. This is not to impugn the sincerity of his professions. Above everything else the abstract merit of his action was determined by what he knew in his sober judgment to be its political inexpediency. When silence would have brought golden reward, he talked. A more neutral attitude would have made him the logical candidate in 1912, for he was the only leader who might then have healed the breaches in the party and carried it once more to victory. But this neutrality was impossible for a man of his temperament to observe. A curious complex of circumstances, beginning over personal grounds, had led him, step by step, farther than he would have wished, to take a position of frank antithesis to Taft, until this made him, against every instinct of wisdom, jeopardize reputation and sacrifice success for principles which he adopted with a sudden fury and afterward even more quickly discarded. Roosevelt's conduct is inexplicable on any mere ground of political ambition or love of office. The greatness of his mistake offers the most convincing proof of the sincerity of his belief.

After the defeat of 1910, he wrote to his future biographer, J. B. Bishop, to explain why he had refrained from saying that he would not be a candidate in 1912. Roosevelt did not wish to put himself in the position where he would be obliged to shirk if it should become his plain duty to accept, and severely criticized Taft for having wrecked the party. Roosevelt then expected to be asked to take command of the sinking ship, yet knew he must face the resentment of many people who would regard him as treacherous to Taft.

He had accurately diagnosed the situation, forecast impending defeat, and practically admitted that in spite of this he wanted to make the fight. An instinct within him and a confidence in his own star compelled his movements and possessed his soul. Already at the Saratoga Convention in 1910, friends who had watched him closely for years were struck by the 'Roosevelt fighting face' which they had never before seen. Even on that political platform where his interests were only indirectly touched, he produced on spectators an impression of pugnacious strength which one of these has described as conveying the suggestion of the cave man with his club on his shoulder going forth to seek and seize his woman.[10]

More by accident than design, he advanced a highly controversial issue which could easily have

been avoided, and aspired to the Presidency, not
merely because he wanted this office again, but because it was the only one worth the fight. As soon as
the demands on Roosevelt to run as a candidate in
1912 became insistent enough to justify his own
inclination, his half-hearted resistance subsided.
During four years he had toyed with the idea, always
leaving a loophole. Now he merely asked as a formal
condition that his nomination should come in response
to a genuine popular demand and not be the result of
an intrigue. These conditions he knew were only
empty words. Behind them stood his belief that
Taft could not be reëlected, and that even if he could
be, his reëlection would prove a misfortune. He
wanted to regard his own nomination as a sacrifice,
and he wanted this sacrifice to come as the result of
yielding to direct pressure. The nomination was to be
forced upon him and people made to know that he
had nothing to gain and much to lose by once more
running for office.

The ostensible reason for the breach came as the
result of La Follette's physical breakdown while
making a speech at Philadelphia early in February,
1912. When, after this, the Senator began by releas-
ing his supporters, some of these hastened at once to
Oyster Bay to plead with Roosevelt that, unless he
should take the leadership, the Progressive cause
would fall to pieces. A week later, a letter signed by
the Republican Governors of seven States requested
him to become a candidate for the Presidency. The
seven Governors insisted that in making this request
they were not considering his personal interests, but

those of the people, and that any refusal would show him unresponsive to a plain public duty. His enemies called this letter a political 'frame-up' inspired by the Colonel, who may have suggested the step, although its significance was no less eloquent. Two days later, President Taft, in a speech at the Republican Club in New York, attacked the extremists who wanted to hurry the country into a condition which had 'no parallel except in the French Revolution or in that babbling anarchy that once characterized the South American Republics. Such extremists are not progressive; they are political emotionalists or neurotics.'

For months Roosevelt had been seething inwardly, unable to hold in restraint the overflow of fierce energy within him or to find an appropriate escape for this. For months he had been uncertain and perplexed as to his course. The conflict of motives, the struggle between the politician and the statesman, between judgment and instinct, had tortured his mind and turned it into a fiery cauldron which left him without rest. Now his fighting spirit was up, and no reason could thwart his rush. The breach was inevitable, for the force within him was too great to have simmered into quiescence. The three events which took place within ten February days — first, the demand made on him after the physical collapse of La Follette, then the round robin of the seven Governors, and lastly the taunts of Taft at the 'political emotionalist' and 'neurotic' — precipitated the struggle and justified Roosevelt in his own mind in making a fight which had become inevitable. After this the lid was off, and on February 21 he announced that 'My hat is in the ring.'

In Roosevelt's speech at Columbus the next day the defiance of his platform also forced a break with the regulars, from whom he had nothing more to hope. He reaffirmed old views about the trusts and declared himself with added emphasis in favor of the initiative, the referendum, and the recall of judicial decisions.

This speech startled every conservative in the country and gave new weapons to his enemies, who immediately attacked him for advocating mob rule. Many of his warmest supporters now felt that they could no longer follow him in his extreme opinions. His closest personal friend, Senator Lodge, 'miserably unhappy,' as he wrote privately to Roosevelt, issued a public statement to declare that he was opposed to the constitutional changes advocated in the speech at Columbus, but in view of his close friendship proposed taking no part whatever in the campaign for the Presidential nomination. Men like Root and George Meyer might have supported Roosevelt until this speech. Others like Colonel Nelson, of the 'Kansas City Star,' privately declared that they were for Roosevelt right or wrong, and refused to admit even to themselves that they didn't approve of anything he did.

The die was cast by Roosevelt without regard for his own fortunes. As a politician he understood that by tearing his party in two he was breaking every rule. The statesman in him appreciated that he was placing in jeopardy the estimate of his public achievement and risking his treasured place in history. He knew that the probabilities were against his nomination and that his election by a divided party was out of question. Yet he persevered, pushed forward by a mystical sense which then caused him to regard himself as the champion of the people's cause. It was magnificent, but it was not war!

IV

With his hat in the ring, the contest was nominally between Roosevelt and Taft, but the latter was willing to take only a secondary and reluctant part in the campaign. His natural aversion to a struggle of this nature, particularly with a former friend, and the little confidence he felt in his own reëlection, restrained him to hold aloof in Presidential dignity. Willingly he would have stepped aside, but the organization could not allow him to do this.

From the start the fight promised to be bitter between Roosevelt and the Old Guard. There exists an odd formalism about our party procedure as soon as the machine finds itself obliged to step into the open and speak in the name of popular approval. Usually the rivalry between candidates intent to capture delegates for the nomination is fought out in such a way that the organization can maintain a kind of neutrality until after the selection of the nominee has been made, but in this case the struggle was only against Roosevelt.

The Colonel, stepping down from his pedestal, was too experienced a politician not to know that the old-timers then in control, like Senator Penrose, Murray

Crane, and Barnes, who had grown up in politics, would load the dice heavily against him. Former rules made to preserve continuity from one administration to another could enable them to exercise a dominating voice within the National Committee. The frame work of this organization was built around a structure which, nominally representative of the party throughout the entire country, in reality conferred control on a small inside group. The Southern States, which sent two hundred and sixteen delegates to the Convention without being able to produce a single vote in the Electoral College, provided the principal channel through which this was effected. The machine, relying on the solid support of its office-holders, was determined at all costs to prevent Roosevelt from again capturing the Republican nomination.

The fighting instinct in the man had now been aroused. He was in a contest after his own heart, battling against tremendous odds and knowing that almost certain defeat stared him in the face. Only blind faith and superb confidence could justify the self-decreed martyrdom to which he was then rushing against every rule of the political game. Roosevelt always had within him a power of energized faith which was able at the shortest notice to espouse an idea and immediately to ennoble this into a deep-rooted conviction. He was then urged forward by a firm belief in the righteousness of his mission for social justice. The white heat of devotion for a cause which had suddenly grown in his mind made him indifferent to any consequences to himself, and the political folly of his course offered the most convincing justification of

his disinterestedness. Roosevelt, who never deluded
himself in his tactics, but often as to the reason for his
actions, had become convinced that national conditions rendered his part inevitable. He was then wholly
careless as to his own fate. Certain of his speeches,
which, delivered with all the fire of his personality,
aroused his hearers to wild enthusiasm, seem commonplace and redundant when read in cold print.
There remain others in which the genuine emotion of
his eloquence will long survive the occasion for their
delivery. In his career as a statesman and as a man of
letters, he never pronounced words more deserving to
be handed down in letters of gold for future generations than those contained in his address at Carnegie
Hall on March 20, 1912, when he spoke of the need
for leaders of inspired idealism able to kindle the
people with the fire from their burning souls: ' ... The
leader for the time being, whoever he may be, is but
an instrument to be used until broken and then to be
cast aside; and if he is worth his salt, he will care no
more when he is broken than a soldier cares when he is
sent where his life is forfeit in order that the victory
may be won.'

Roosevelt, then, visualizing himself as the martyr
in a great cause, had, however, every intention of
making as good a fight as he knew, in the process of his
own martyrdom. At first his followers were not an
impressive company. Except for the seven Governors
who had urged him to run again and whose influence
could be exerted in their own States, Roosevelt began
his campaign with little more than the enthusiasm
of a few supporters, which, apart from personal

friends, was obtained largely from radicals, parlor socialists, and that 'lunatic fringe' he had so often ridiculed and whose well-intentioned efforts led to his own frequent embarrassment.[11]

The apathy of the public usually provides the politicians' opportunity to control enough disciplined votes to win at the primaries. Roosevelt's only hope at this time lay in his ability to arouse public feeling sufficiently in the thirteen States, mainly Northern and Western, where new legislation providing for direct primary elections had been enacted, and which would allow the members of a party to express their preference for him as their candidate. The agitation for direct primaries was then in full swing, and its impending victory had not yet brought disillusion to those who believed in them as a remedy against the bosses' power. Partly because the idea was popular, and partly to obtain a much-needed publicity when most of the press was against the Colonel, his headquarters proposed that all delegates should be chosen in this manner even in States where, as yet, no legislation had been enacted to provide for them. From every point of view such a suggestion could only be advantageous to Roosevelt, who telegraphed directly to the President asking him to endorse this offer. The Taft managers, who argued the question instead of laughing it into silence, were obliged to print in their own papers the story of a controversy which placed Roosevelt once more before the country as the leader in a popular cause fighting the reactionaries.

In the thirteen States where direct primaries took place, the choice for Roosevelt was overwhelming and impressive. In Illinois, which passed the primary law at a special session of the legislature called for this purpose, only two of the fifty-eight delegates were not for Roosevelt. In Ohio, Taft's native State, the Colonel received an enormous majority, and the same was true in Pennsylvania and California. Wherever a popular expression of opinion was possible, the bosses were repudiated by the voters. Out of 382 delegates chosen at these primaries in the most important Republican States of the Union, 278 were instructed to vote for Roosevelt as their Presidential nominee at the June Convention.

The confidence in the easy victory which the organization promised itself in the early days of the campaign had now been succeeded by nervousness. To beat Roosevelt no longer appeared so simple as the extent of popular enthusiasm behind him became more apparent. Feeling ran to extremes on both sides, for the machine was determined not to allow him to be its candidate. Many then worked themselves into a state bordering on frenzy, in which they portrayed the Colonel as a kind of dangerous anarchist solely intent on destruction. Eye-witnesses have described to the writer how William Barnes, head of the New York machine, represented his own son's education at Harvard as endangered by Roosevelt's election, and he maintained excitedly that the principle of property was at stake; that it was a solemn duty to protect the country from the anarchy which would succeed if Roosevelt again became President. Party success no longer hung in the balance, for Republican defeat by the Democrats had become a foregone conclusion. The cry of the Old Guard was how to save the United States from the ruin which Roosevelt was said to have in mind in his wish to destroy our national institutions.

The fanaticism of a conviction when it is shared by men of determination and resource leads to unscrupulous processes. The opportunity to resort to these came in June, when the roll-call of the Republican Convention which was to nominate the Presidential candidate was made up. After the contested primary elections, there arrived at Chicago rival sets of delegates from different States, each of which clamored for recognition. Two hundred seats were in dispute and the credentials of delegates came up for examination before the National Committee of fifty-three members, which was supposedly representative of the Republican Party throughout the country. Fifteen members of this Committee had already been repudiated by their own States in their efforts to become delegates. Ten others were from the Southern States, not one of which could give an electoral vote, and four were merely organization appointments from the Territories and insular possessions. Yet these twenty-nine members, who represented nothing more than the bedrock party machine, were able to dictate the choice of the candidate of the Republicans. The Committee found means of doing this through its power to recognize only its own delegates, and proceeded with these to make up the temporary roll-call of the Convention. 'Beat Roosevelt' was its battle-cry, as delegate after delegate was hand-picked for this purpose.

The fight lasted for days, first before the Committee, which passed on the delegates' credentials, and afterwards continued on the floor of the Convention. Roosevelt, unable to keep away, came to Chicago, against the entreaties of his friends, some of whom still think that this move cost him the nomination, and his public declaration that he 'would not take it lying down' was received with tumultuous enthusiasm. He had to meet a difficult situation created by his supporters, many of whom, led by Governor Johnson of California, wanted at once to bolt the Convention, because of the flagrant theft of the delegates.[12] They felt convinced that this break would give strength to the Progressive movement through the country. Roosevelt believed, however, that it was more important to make his own record clear to the point at which the Convention would confirm the stolen delegates. Perhaps also the feeling that his enemies would accuse him again of overriding all established practices confirmed him in his wish to do nothing which might lend itself to an illegal interpretation.

On the floor of the Convention the Roosevelt supporters charged fraud against the Old Guard and invectives were freely bandied about till the police had to be called in to maintain order. The seventy-two delegates whose right to sit had been contested were brought in to vote on the temporary organization, and their deciding voice gave Root the chairmanship by a narrow majority, against Governor McGovern, the candidate of the Roosevelt supporters. Five days' fighting, during which time the radical wing repeatedly threatened to bolt, were still necessary in order to complete the organization of the Convention. Root, who had been the most trusted of Roosevelt's advisers when he was President, who was his personal friend, and, although then estranged, afterward became so again, was acting on Taft's side. Repeatedly he gave his decisions as Chairman with questionable fairness but superb skill, which covered the most flagrant rulings with a veneer of legality and a recourse to precedent. Purposely he avoided any mention of Roosevelt's name, since this would have brought about a demonstration in his favor. The principal fight hinged over the rights of delegates, whose credentials were under dispute, to vote on their own status. Root decided that, although they could not do this in their own cases, they would be allowed to vote on the status of others similarly placed, and plausibly based his argument on the ground that otherwise a rump minority could upset any convention. By this decision seventy-two delegates provided an organization majority of seventy-one. The Roosevelt men were not recognized, ostensibly on the ground that their choice had been improperly made.

All this time, behind the scenes, the Old Guard was putting out feelers toward a compromise candidate. Providing they could down Roosevelt, they felt indifferent over Taft. Yet it was self-evident that Roosevelt's support was necessary if there was to be any possibility of electing a Republican in November. At one time a proposal for the nomination was made to Governor Hadley, who led the Colonel's forces on the floor of the Convention. The genuineness of the Old Guard's offer, made behind the scenes, was open to doubt, and the prior condition laid down by Roosevelt to purge of fraud the roll of delegates made any compromise then impossible. The Old Guard could not consent to this, and preferred accepting certain defeat to subscribing to an admission of its wrongdoing, the immediate effect of which would have been to throw the nomination to Roosevelt. The latter, although taking the position that he would support the candidacy of any one selected by the Convention after its roll-call had been amended, knew well that in this event no other candidate than himself was possible. Yet personal ambition was then far from being his only motive. A witness has described the overtures made by a group of delegates who came eager to take steps which might have resulted in his nomination. He rejected these instantly, because they did not include purging the roll-call. Deliberately by insisting on this condition he threw away every political chance.[13]

When his own delegates had finally been eliminated, Roosevelt came out with a direct charge of fraud. 'The Convention,' he wrote, 'has now declined to purge the roll of the fraudulent delegates placed thereon by the defunct National Committee, and the majority which thus endorsed fraud was made a majority only because it included the fraudulent delegates themselves, who all sat as judges on one another's cases.... This action makes the Convention in no proper sense any longer a Republican Convention representing the real Republican Party.... It represents nothing but successful fraud in overriding the will of the rank and file of the Party. Any man nominated by the Convention as now constituted would be merely the beneficiary of this successful fraud.'

V

Few people believed that Roosevelt, having been defeated in the Convention, would be prepared to break with the Republicans in order to form a new party of his own. No other American would have dared to do this. The breach in party loyalty by a man signally honored with its favors was unprecedented in the annals of our political history. The writer recalls the owner of a great newspaper speaking of Roosevelt, several years later, in terms of opprobrium because of this. From the standpoint of political opportunism, the break seemed suicidal. He knew he could not win and that Taft was certain to go down to defeat. He knew, after the Convention was over, that even a perfunctory endorsement of the latter's candidacy would make him the logical nominee of a united party in 1916. Instead, he accepted insult and disaster to commit the one unforgivable sin of our politics and tear asunder the party of which he had been the leader.

Amid scenes which resembled a religious crusade, a meeting was hastily organized by the Colonel's followers. Roosevelt announced in its presence that he was in the fight for principles of which the most important went back to Sinai and was contained in the Commandment, 'Thou shalt not steal.... Thou shalt not steal a nomination.... Thou shalt not steal from the people the birthright of the people to rule themselves.'

In spite of moral maxims there remained only one slim chance for success. If the Democratic Party was also to split asunder in the same way as the Republican, Roosevelt might still be elected, perhaps, with Bryan's support. The latter had been a spectator at the Chicago Republican Convention and had had there a number of private talks with Roosevelt. It was known that he would not accept Champ Clark, who then seemed likely to be the Democratic nominee. But Bryan's influence was sufficiently powerful at the Baltimore Democratic Convention ten days later to prevent the nomination from going to Champ Clark, and he remained within the fold. After that, Roosevelt, though instinctively clutching at hope for the impossible, was never under any real illusion as to his own defeat.

A National Progressive Convention was called to meet at Chicago early in August in the same hall in which Roosevelt had made his fight. An enthusiasm which emanated from a deep conviction of the loftiness of their mission characterized the proceedings of the delegates, who as they assembled sang 'Onward, Christian Soldiers.' Roosevelt professed his readiness to support any nominee, but it was well known that the Convention met for no other purpose than to select him. His phrase, 'We stand at Armageddon and we battle for the Lord,' marked the fervor of the assemblage in which the Bull Moose Party was founded.

The idea of a new Progressive Party is said to have been proposed at a dinner given to Gifford Pinchot at St. Paul, in June, 1910. Pinchot, who had been intimately associated with Roosevelt over Conservation, continued to see much of him after his own break with Taft. Personal grounds also with Pinchot had added bitterness growing out of differences as to questions of public policy which had arisen over the grant of Government lands. Roosevelt had not been averse to seeing one of his close friends take a position of open feud with the Administration before he himself had been ready to assume a similar stand. Pinchot's influence, personal and political, over Roosevelt was perhaps less great than some had assumed, but it fell on a soil already prepared, for the break with Taft had from the start been inevitable.

At the end of February, 1912, after his speech at Columbus, Roosevelt had spent an evening with two old friends, William Roscoe Thayer, the biographer, and Judge Robert Grant, at the latter's house in Boston. Roosevelt had then expressed the wish 'to draw into one dominant stream all the intelligent and patriotic elements in order to prepare against the social upheaval which will otherwise overwhelm us.' The most important questions of the day seemed to him to be the humanitarian and economic problems, and he affirmed that reforms had become urgent, as the will of the people had been thwarted, especially by the courts. He recognized that his own motives were complex. He admitted to his friends that he liked power, but cared nothing to be President merely for the sake of the office.[14]

All this was true, and there is no reason to seek for a more subtle explanation of his conduct. Progressivism made a natural appeal to Roosevelt on social,

political, and personal grounds. He found in it
a natural channel to express his real sympathy with
the downtrodden which was of ancient date and
justified him in putting himself forward as their
leader. It responded to his belief in a strong government, able in the interest of the entire community to
regulate the great corporations which had organized
our business and to exercise a control over public
franchises. In his mind Progressivism meant an intelligent direction undertaken for the general welfare
of the community by the State, which could brook no
rival. Politically, also, he welcomed in the Progressive
programme a more immediate response to the people's
wishes. Instead of their desires being filtered and
diverted through devious channels, and retarded by
checks on legislation or court decisions rendered under
the influence of a narrow interpretation of property
rights, he discerned new opportunities ahead of him
which made for leadership in a democracy. He saw
the people prepared to rise to overthrow the bosses
and follow an inspired chief. Had he not declared
that personally he was ready to accept any such
leader? But no other had yet appeared, and whenever he expressed his willingness to efface himself in
favor of some one else who could advance these
cherished principles, his supporters merely smiled.

Unconsciously also many personal motives had
made him a Progressive. Was it possible to adjust his
exuberant vitality to the slow and cautious step of
the organization and tread behind men he despised,
merely because they directed its workings. Silence
or negative acquiescence was out of the question with

one of Roosevelt's nature. Better a thousand times to be defeated and perish in a worthy cause than to drag on a cautiously timorous existence. It was, in a slightly different form, the same problem which had repeatedly confronted him in his early days in New York. He felt the same cherished wish for a direct response of the people to his sense of leadership and the same indignation at the anonymous block of politicians who stood across his virtuous path.

With the Presidency behind him, with no longer any particular wish for office by itself but only for the power it conferred, his restless energy and instinct for domination spurred him forward to find in life a great adventure, which he enriched with the picturesqueness of a vivid imagination, which he ennobled with the vision of an ideal, and which he hoped to traverse fighting to the end. What meaning, after all, could old party ties offer him, with their sterile limitations and their atmosphere of cautious compromise, compared to the promise of a cause which was henceforth to be his own. Faced by the certainty of defeat but with the joy of battle before him, he became the Progressive candidate to lead the fight with all his vigor against what he denounced as the old corrupt party machines.

His address before the Convention of the new party in Chicago on August 6, 1912, was typical of the battling Roosevelt, violent in the attack on his enemies, sonorous in the declaration of truisms, picturesque in his description of the organization's plunder league, but moderate also in the defense of principles which he had espoused somewhat hastily and was perhaps already beginning to regret. Along with the measures of social welfare he advocated, it was still necessary to stand by the initiative, referendum, and recall, but he did not attempt to dogmatize about how these reforms should be achieved. He proclaimed that to utilize such measures indiscriminately would cause disaster; they were to be held in reserve to arrest the misdeeds of public servants only when it became evident that these could not be corrected in normal fashion. Such professions were not very radical. Nine tenths of what he said could have been declared at almost any time in his public career. The remaining few ideas which the campaign had brought to the fore were already being modified, though even in their attenuated form these were to cost him thousands of votes.

The Progressive Party exists no more, but many of its ideas were later introduced into the platform of the other parties. Yet the campaign gave Roosevelt occasion for a magnificent display of fighting energy as he toured through the country arousing popular enthusiasm wherever he went. Bitterly attacked by his adversaries, the violence of the newspaper criticism leveled at him is said to have caused a madman to shoot him three weeks before the election, just as he was about to make a speech at Milwaukee. The bullet lodged in the chest, broke a rib, and made a serious wound, which would have been fatal if its course had not been deflected by his iron spectacle case and the folded manuscript of his speech. Roosevelt had the habit, common to many men in public life, of having his manuscripts prepared on small sheets with extra spacing between the lines, and this one was folded into a hundred sheets of heavy paper through which the bullet had to pass.[15]

In spite of the advice of physicians and the entreaties of his friends, he insisted on proceeding to the hall to make his address. 'It may be the last one I shall ever deliver, but I am going to deliver this one!' he exclaimed; and to the audience he said, 'It takes more than that to kill a bull moose.' Nothing could stop him, and for one hour and a half he spoke till, approaching the end of his speech, he was plainly weakening. Not till it was over would he allow himself to be taken by special train to Chicago to be operated upon.

The indomitable courage which he then displayed fitted in with his reasoned philosophy of life. On his way to the hospital he related to a friend that when he had left for the Cuban campaign he had realized that he might be shot, but made up his mind that if he were and the shock did not stop him, he would go straight on no matter what happened to him afterward. Later, this rule appealed to him as a maxim of conduct.[16] It was no mere instinct which made him proceed with his speech, but a series of reasoned processes. To Sir Edward Grey, who wrote him to express sympathy, he explained his motives with the utmost frankness. As soon as he felt that he had been shot, he put his hands to his lips to see if there was any blood. As there was none, he realized that the chances were twenty to one that the wound would not be fatal. After taking steps to protect the would-be assassin from being lynched, he felt that his next duty was to make the speech, for in the unlikely event of the wound being mortal he wished to die with his boots on. Always it had seemed to him that the best way to die was in the act of doing something worth while, whether leading a regiment or anything else. And if he were to perish at such a time, it would be difficult thereafter for people to question his sincerity.[17]

His philosophy of life was contained in this explanation: Reasoned courage, audacity, fortitude, moderation, and the instinct to lift daily existence out of its drabness by exploits of valor. The spectacular element which made this incident unique in the career of any public man was no calculated effect, but formed part of his stride. Behind it all, hardly expressed, yet sorely tormenting him, was the haunting knowledge that many then doubted the sincerity of his political motives. He had winced in silence under the grossness of the attacks against him. In this speech, which might be his last, he had occasion to prove to the American people that no element of selfish ambition entered into what, perhaps, were to be his dying words. Motives of different order flashed across his mind to reënforce a decision which his courage alone would in any event have dictated. Behind it all, unmentioned even to his intimates, was his wish to stand well before posterity. As if his act was not enough, he preserved copies of his letters analyzing his feelings over this incident for his biographer to publish. An invariable practice caused him to retain copies of everything he wrote, both for reference and for his position in history.

The appraisal of earthly glories he had long since

made. He would go on fighting so long as he lived in order to find outlet for the overwhelming sense of leadership which struggled within him, but his ambition henceforth was not merely for office and hardly for any particular principle, though in his mind this provided the justifying excuse for his conduct. His real ambition was for his remembrance as a man to stand out in immortal fame for future generations.

VI

A few years after his defeat, Roosevelt writing to his son admitted that it might have been better after he left the Presidency if he had taken no part in politics. In the next sentence of the letter he characteristically justified all he had done. How could he preach virtue in the abstract unless ready to apply it in concrete cases? When men of high character appealed to him for help, he would have shirked his duty had he remained indifferent.[18]

It was easy to find ennobling motives for his conduct and identify this with the practice of virtue, but as a politician Roosevelt knew that he had backed the wrong horse. He had often been fond of describing himself as a practical idealist. This practical side made him understand at once that, although the Republican Party could survive any defeat, this was not the case with the Progressive. The campaign was hardly over before Roosevelt had realized that there was no future ahead for the Bull Moose. Four million votes cast for him meant a personal success scored over Taft, but were poor compensation for the knowledge that the country had grown tired of his leadership. The people had refused to be lifted out of their sodden materialism or be alarmed by the startling picture of national depravity which his speeches had so vividly described.

In the sober awakening which followed the excitement of the election, Roosevelt found ample time to take stock of his new position, and the prospect was not encouraging. Defeat at once made him more critical of those who had supported him, and in turn these became more critical of him. The small Progressive group in Congress obeyed no leadership and their feeling against bossism was extreme enough to make many of these resent having even Roosevelt as their boss. In sadness he found that the Progressive cause had attracted emotional cranks of all kinds, who urged him to take up the most harebrained schemes. During the flush of the campaign, in the fever of battle, their eccentricities had not impressed him with such disagreeable force. In the chastened hour of defeat, the real conservatism of Roosevelt's character, which was greater than he would have admitted, inwardly revolted at the freakish radicalism displayed by many of his partisans. He was ready to throw overboard not a little of the Progressive baggage, for the fervor of his convictions had already become less ardent. Hardly a fortnight after the election, he began to show what his official biographer has called 'a disposition to abandon the issue' of the recall of judges, which never again excited his interest. Before long he was prepared to go still further and abandon the leadership of the Progressive Party, with the vague feeling of satisfaction that in one way or another its principles would triumph. 'I have to continue to take a certain interest in it until a new man of sufficient power comes along,' he wrote to an English friend.[19] But this interest was henceforth not excessive.

Instinctively he shrank from any longer asserting himself in the Progressive Party councils. With seeming disinterestedness and with a semblance of his customary vigor, he still maintained that he would fight in the ranks so long as he lived for the cause and the platform for which he had fought in 1912. Beyond declarations of this nature, he did not overexert himself, and justified his abstention with the argument that action on his part would be construed into the belief that he was still aspiring to some leadership in the movement and would thereby do it harm. For once he preferred to be less conspicuous. 'When it is evident that a leader's day is past, the one service he can render is to step aside and leave the ground clear for the development of a successor. It seems to me that such is the case now as regards myself.' [20]

There was nothing that he wanted less than the leadership of the Bull Moose. He had led one forlorn hope, but the glamour of the cause had vanished with his previous enthusiasm, and he found little to attract him in a continuous martyrdom suffered among irresponsible cranks. More and more he felt out of sympathy with the Progressive Party, though still making speeches in its behalf. The time soon came when he even took pleasure 'in the smash that came to the Progressive Party... the reformers tended to go into sheer lunacy.' [21] At least he would no longer be hampered by the extravagance of his reformer friends.

The mercurial quality in his temperament had sunk to its lowest depth. To himself he seemed a solitary figure, who, after having enjoyed a commanding position in the world, had broken with the great Republican organization through which he had risen to eminence, and no longer cared to remain with a new and shapeless party with whose multifarious aims he had ceased to sympathize after he had vainly tried to lead it. The fact that a Democratic administration was in office completed his isolation. He still retained the affection of a few enthusiastic supporters, but knew that he had lost his grip on the public interest. The country no longer cared for what he said or did, and it was galling to be made to realize the extent to which he had shrunk for the time from its outlook. The writer recalls a visit he paid to him early in 1913, when they spoke together of the imminence of a great European war. The writer dwelt on the necessity for America to arm with this in view and expressed regret that he had been unable to find a publisher in the United States for an article advocating preparedness, which he had been obliged to print in London. Roosevelt, who in his customary emphatic manner declared that he agreed with every word of the article, remarked also that he was not surprised at the lack of interest taken. He gave as an illustration that he himself had made an important address before the American Historical Association, yet no attention whatever had been paid to this by our press. The address was on 'History as Literature,' and it was the man of letters in Roosevelt who spoke. But the man of letters in America commands attention only when he is a sensational or a public figure, and Roosevelt had then passed out of popular interest. At this time he sadly felt that 'the people as a whole are heartily tired of me and of my aims.'[22]

He could only mark time, filling out his days as best he knew over a period, the end of which he could not foresee nor feel that there would again be anything left for him to accomplish. The stirring events with which he had been associated, the country's forward march which he had headed with his great stride, the Nation's affectionate applause, the world's admiration, had all become memories of the past to which he could never more look forward. The overflow of his energy no longer found its outlet. He knew that he was only repeating the lot of every great popular leader since the beginning of history, who after rising to high eminence had later fallen low. His courage and his pride alike refused to admit that there was any peculiar tragedy in his fate. Self-pity ran counter to all his philosophy of life. Nor did he find in himself the ground to complain of fortune. Possessing attainments which with ruthless self-analysis he disparagingly described as mediocre, lacking the flash of genius, he yet had risen to the most conspicuous position attained by any living human being of his time. He had brought rare distinction to his name for his descendants to enjoy and had written his deeds large in American history. Could any man do more? It was only human if some silent rancor then gnawed his soul to revolt against the feeling of being dead before his time.

Better than any one, he knew, amid the silence around him, that in his isolation he possessed the same abilities, the same overwhelming vitality and power of leadership which only a few years before had made him the idol of the American people.

Doubtless this feeling was not foreign to the journey of exploration he then undertook in Brazil. Roosevelt desired to get away from a political atmosphere in which he could no longer take part, and forget. The early tastes of the naturalist reasserted themselves and induced him to embark on the terrible journey through the hardly known regions of Central Brazil, to give his name to a river and to experience sufferings which then imperiled his life and later sapped his health — for never again did he recover his full strength. At one time, sorely bruised in the leg, which had become badly inflamed, and feeling that he was an impediment to his companions in their difficult progress through the jungle, he thought of suicide. His health had been seriously undermined and he was too enfeebled by sickness even to splash water on his face. He resisted the temptation of self-destruction as soon as he realized that his son would never abandon his remains in the tropical wilderness.[23] Later, as he related this incident, he added that, except for the separation from his family, death meant little to him. After the fullness of his life and the bitterness of recent experience, what could there still be in store?

He returned to Sagamore Hill for a different homecoming from the one which had greeted him after his African journey. No longer were there public

rejoicings or welcome save from close friends. He
lived a family life and professed to find happiness
in this. He read much; he wrote not a little. His
voyage to the Amazon was followed by a book,
'Through the Brazilian Wilderness.' He tried to
discover new values in old pursuits, for there were
few things with which at one time or another he had
not occupied himself.

VII

On June 15, 1914, Mr. Bryan, then Secretary of
State, telegraphed to inform the Greek Minister of
Foreign Affairs that President Wilson's peace plan
had been accepted in principle by thirty-four nations,
among which were Germany, Austria, France, Great
Britain, and Italy. Two months later, on August 14,
and ten days after hostilities had broken out, Mr.
Bryan telegraphed to our Ambassadors in Paris and
in London that eighteen of his peace treaties had been
ratified on the previous day. The Administration in
Washington still paid little attention to a World War.

Beyond a proposal of good offices telegraphed to
London on July 28, it is difficult to discover any
further contribution made by Mr. Wilson in the way
of efforts to preserve peace. It may be idle specu-
lating what a more competent diplomacy could have
achieved, but Roosevelt has recorded his own opinion
on this subject. In private talk he stated it as his
belief, not without some reason, that it would have
been possible to delay, at least for a time, the declaration of war by calling an international conference,
and that we ought to have helped Sir Edward Grey

in his efforts to postpone hostilities until such a conference could have met. Roosevelt was convinced that Cleveland and McKinley would have done this, and he mentioned to a friend that he should have felt himself a criminal if he had failed to bring about this delay. He blamed the disaster which had befallen the world, a little too exclusively, on the incompetence of the Administration at Washington.[24]

When in those last days of July, peace and war hung in the balance, it is probable that a President as well informed and resourceful as Roosevelt, with the prestige of his authority and knowing how to utilize a trained diplomatic service, could have accomplished much. After the results he had been able to achieve by personal means at Algeciras and in the Russo-Japanese negotiations, it is difficult to imagine Roosevelt standing passively by in the world calamity. To his friend of many years, the British Ambassador, Sir Cecil Spring Rice, he wrote in confidence of what steps he would have taken had he then been President.[25] As the head of a power which had signed the Hague Treaties, he would have claimed the right to call attention to the guaranty of Belgium's neutrality. He would have declared that he accepted these treaties as imposing an obligation which not only the United States but all neutral nations should join in confirming. Nor would he have made such a statement unless willing to back it up, though he believed that if he had been President, the American people would have followed him.

But he was not President, with the opportunity for leadership resting on popularity, trust, and power that the office conferred. His following had dwindled, his prestige had shrunk, and in isolation he saw around him mainly the dark shadows of a shattered authority. To announce flamboyantly what he would have done had he been in the White House, to explain the diplomatic steps he would have taken in those critical days before the outbreak of the war, to express his indignation over the violation of Belgium, would have been, in his own words, 'mere clamor and nothing more.'

Roosevelt's writings at the outbreak of the war were singularly restrained and in a sense not unfavorable to the Germans. In the light of the attitude he was soon to take, his early hesitations are a little difficult to understand and were later held up against him. Were these solely due, as he declared, to his wish not to embarrass Wilson's policy of neutrality? May there not also have been a lurking feeling that he had lost touch with the American people and confidence in himself, and in his uncertainty was unwilling to take too pronounced a position? He had just passed through a chastening purgatory, during which he had been forced to realize the fickleness of public favor and to verify the sinister predictions he had made at the moment of his greatest popularity. After vainly taking up one cause, he had little wish again to associate himself with failure. Moreover, personal friends and supporters entreated him not to touch Wilson's foreign policy.[26] Was it unnatural for him to feel reluctant to assume a public attitude which, unaccompanied by responsibility or any direct power of action and without countervail-

ing advantage, would only bring on him the hatred
of pacifists, pro-Germans, and the vast majority of
the indifferent who were over-glad to follow Wilson's
precepts?

At the outbreak of the war, the writer had written
an article in which he called attention to the probable
consequences to the United States of a German
victory, and advocated immediate preparedness as
the only means for escaping our later intervention.
He had then asked Roosevelt to write a preface for this
with a view to its publication, but the latter refused
at the time, though he was to do so later,[27] on the
ground that it went further than he was ready to go.
His position was still somewhat hesitant. In the
letter to Spring Rice he had expressed as his personal
conviction that the majority of the American people
stood behind Wilson, and he added that in a crisis
of this nature few could be expected to make up their
minds for themselves and rightly tended to support
the President.

In these words, written to a friend, lies the answer
to the controversy as to whether the United States
was ready for war before 1917. With Wilson, then,
preaching neutrality in deed and thought, the country
certainly preferred to follow the more comfortable
path. Amid doubts and hesitations, amid the blast
and counterblast of rival propaganda, the great body
of American opinion, perplexed and better acquainted
with facts than able to read their causes or consequences, found no shelter of convincing leadership
behind which it could form. At a moment when the
moral unity of the Nation had more than ever become

imperative, and the necessity for preparedness had
become self-evident, the negative indecision of the
Administration under color of neutrality encouraged
the deep rifts brought about by opposing sympathies
to widen beneath the surface.

Roosevelt had begun by regarding Wilson as an
adroit man and a good speaker, though he thought
him lacking in conviction. Soon he condemned
Democratic policy in Mexico and toward the World
War, and the opportunities then missed by Wilson
became heart-breaking to Roosevelt. 'How I wish
I were President at this moment!' he wrote to Baron
Rosen, who had been a Russian envoy at the Portsmouth Conference.[28] Boyishly Roosevelt declared
he would be willing to accept the Presidency with a
guaranty of being removed from it just as soon as he
had succeeded in doing what he had started out to
accomplish. He felt how immeasurably better his
own handling would have been. Never before did
he have occasion to regret so deeply his failure in
1912.

Political motives had induced him to refrain from
attacking Wilson till after the fall elections in 1914,
but indignation was bubbling within him.[29] 'Upon
my word, Wilson and Bryan are the very worst men
we have ever had in their positions,' he wrote to
Lodge.[30] The storm raging inside soon found occasion to burst into violence. When news of the sinking
of the Lusitania was received, Roosevelt came out
with a vigorous denunciation of murder on the high
seas. It was the old Roosevelt once more, freed from
all restraints, feeling that at last the convincing

offense had come to unleash his wrath. No longer was silence necessary, no longer did he have to equivocate in platitudes or follow another hated leader. Henceforth his own voice would be heard in all its indignation. Henceforth he was once more going to assume an independent leadership. As if better to bring out the contrast between the two men, on the day following Roosevelt's indictment of the Germans, President Wilson addressed an audience of naturalized citizens with the famous words, 'There is such a thing as a man being too proud to fight.'

Soon Roosevelt's action ran along parallel though closely adjacent lines. He had openly taken a position against Germany which could only lead to war. This attitude required a moral and material preparedness in America which there were as yet no indications of the Wilson Administration bringing about. Already before the sinking of the Lusitania, Roosevelt had begun preaching unhyphenated Americanism. It had long been a favorite subject of his, on which he could point to a record of twenty years. Time and again he had publicly upheld an undiluted Americanism which took no heed of race or creed. Possibly he was a little inclined to overemphasize these elements in order to insist on the extent to which he disregarded them. With spoken and written word he then addressed the country and began to build up a body of opinion which was immensely to assist the popular readiness for our entrance into the war. Many have seen in his effort the highest public service he has rendered, and it is not impossible that this will appear even greater in

the decades to come than it did in the years of the
Great War. When Roosevelt pointed out that Americanism rests neither on ancestry nor creed, but lies
in the meaning of the spirit, he was holding up a
truer ideal for future generations to reverence. His
words will live after many of the half-baked assumptions, made in the name of Science, to fit the fashions
of the day, shall have been forgotten.

The stand he then took against the hyphenated
Americans who looked to their Old-World origins
in order to explain German sympathies was based
on the ground that there was room for only one
allegiance in America. His argument was elementary
and direct, often personal by its example. He drew
attention to the different strains, even of German
blood in his own veins, to bring out that he was plain
American, but also to allow many an immigrant to
feel an indefinite kinship with him, however remote.
Arguments of present and future importance to the
country's welfare were developed by him in elemental
terms. Humorously he defended the frequent obviousness of his statement with the remark that the
public, unable to take in the fine lines of an etching,
needed a circus poster. Patriotism, preparedness,
moral and physical, with its political and military
corollaries, now occupied his mind. He realized that
the future evolution of America was being decided
and that the effect of what would then be done must
be felt for generations to come. All the time his
indignation grew over the fact that in a crisis of
momentous consequence the power should rest with
Wilson, who with soft, plausible words was able

to lull the American people into a comfortable indifference travestied under nobler designations. Once
more, Roosevelt was in full revolt.

VIII

Roosevelt never liked Barnes, the leader of the
Republican organization in New York, who in 1912
had fought him bitterly, and three years later had
unsuccessfully brought suit for libel against him.
Yet, as he wrote to Lodge, he preferred even Barnes
to Wilson. His own plans were already laid. 'The
Republican Party *must* be more amenable to reason'
and make it easy for Progressives like himself to get
the others back of him in the fight to drive Wilson
and Bryan from power.[31] Henceforth a good part of
his ambition was to lead the Bull Moose into the
Republican fold. This maneuver required skill to
perform, for he had no wish to be alone when he
crossed the lines. The Colonel did not intend to
separate himself from his Progressives unless there
developed a 'vital national crisis.'

Of course Roosevelt wanted the Republican nomination in 1916. But this neither misled him as to his
chances nor induced him to try to catch the wind.
When suggestions were made that the Republicans
might think of nominating him, he wrote that if they
did so it would be because of their certainty that he
would be defeated and wanted to get him perma-
nently out of the way.[32] The people, he still felt, were
not only opposed to his policies, but against him personally, and he found the opinion widespread that
he was acting out of motives of selfish ambition with-

out regard for the good of the country. He then thought that nine tenths of the men of influence in New York, big and little, were bitterly opposed to him.

He derived some satisfaction from his own martyr-dom. For Roosevelt, the bottom of the pit also held out attractions. At a time when he had never been more convinced of the righteousness of his cause or of his own disinterestedness, his motives were being denounced as unworthy. He knew that he had run somewhat ahead of the American people in discover-ing the war. The further fact that he was then being reviled, far from causing him misgivings as to his conduct, made him all the firmer in his attitude and left any heart-burnings that he felt merely for de-ploring the inadequacy of popular understanding.

This position reflected credit on him. He was no longer ambitious to secure high office for its own sake. He still wanted to become President, perhaps more than ever, with war imminent, but, conscious of his own future fame, he desired this only if the country should be ready to rise to his expectations. Deep down he understood that his nomination was most unlikely. For him publicly to express the wish not to be a candidate unless the country ac-cepted his ideas was an obvious truism, for the wind had to veer sharply in his direction before his chance could come. He was also right to seek the Presidency only at his own price. Already in the 1912 Republican Convention, he had assumed an unyielding attitude which may have cost him the nomination. At that time he had not yet faced real adversity. Now, de-

pressed after his chastening experience and with the
sense of impending age hanging over him, he felt
more than a doubt that the White House would ever
again lie within his reach. The statesman and the
patriot also had gained mastery in his heart to keep
down the politician's instincts, and the ambitions he
still entertained were shaped by higher motives than
ever before. The position he then assumed admitted
of no compromise, no silence over what he proposed
to do, or pledge, avowed or implied. His attitude had
to be made clear before the country, and while with
all his heart he hoped that the people might follow
him, his judgment left him with few illusions.

Yet the beginning of a drift in his direction was
already becoming noticeable. Lodge, who was never
misled by his friendship, discovered signs of its rapid
growth, and this without management or artifice.
The only question was whether the current could
become swift enough to make itself felt in time to
influence the primaries. Lodge agreed with Roosevelt in thinking that a nomination fought for would
not be worth having.

In March, 1916, from Trinidad in the West Indies,
Roosevelt issued a statement of his position. After
declaring, with the usual denials, that he would not
enter into any fight for the nomination to be made in
his behalf, he added that it would be a mistake to
select him as a candidate 'unless the country has in
its mood something of the heroic.'

This was honest politics. With the remembrance
of 1912 and the bitterness of partisan feeling which
still prevailed, with the animosity of the hyphenated

aroused against him, Roosevelt understood that
unless public opinion favored intervention, he could
not be the most suitable candidate. He had already
made known his attitude over our participation in
the war, and to have assumed any different position
at this time would have exposed him to the charge
of equivocating and weakened his power of leadership.
He wanted to make clear that if there was ambition
implied in his conduct, it was an ambition which ran
counter to all the political craft of which he was a
master and attached itself solely to what he saw was
the country's honor and good. In defiance of every
consideration of political sagacity, in the two months
preceding the Convention he went West to talk
national preparedness and denounce German atro-
cities in the very cities in which the German element
was strongest.

It was his old audacity, patriotically and intelli-
gently used. He knew that his sole chance lay in
persuading the country to rise to the occasion and
again follow him as its leader. Admittedly it was the
slimmest hope, but it was the only one which consci-
entiously he could entertain. He refused to compromise in order to increase his chance by angling in less
resolute waters.

The contest he made was for a cause after his own
heart. He advanced fewer of the generalities and
none of the accommodations with which, under a
surface of adamant he had been ready enough in
former years to qualify his stand so long as he had
discussed capital and labor or drawn careful balances
between good and bad trusts.

The immediate goal was to turn out the Democratic Administration because of its inability to
defend American lives or honor. The issue he raised
was over preparedness for war by a country determined to assert its rights and avenge the murder of
its citizens on the high seas. He was anxious to
attack, but had no wish to lead a forlorn hope, and
was apprehensive over what he scented as 'pussy-
footing' in the attitude of the Republicans. Their
tactics, he thought, were mapped out to beat Wilson
by keeping neutral as to international duty, support-
ing him in what seemed to Roosevelt a sham preparedness programme and trusting to the tariff and
some understanding with the German vote to defeat
him. All this might be good politics, but left the
Colonel without interest as to whether Wilson or
some one else was elected, and he foresaw that without a clearer issue most of the Progressives would
even support Wilson.[33] Whether alone or in company,
his own stand was going to remain uncompromising.
He would have to wait to see whether the country
would in time catch up.

The Progressive organization under the management of George W. Perkins tried at first to induce the
Republicans to select Roosevelt as their candidate in
1916. Purely as a tactical measure the Bull Moose
proposed to hold their convention, also in Chicago,
at the same time that the Republican Convention
was to meet. In the background existed the idea to
use this as a club, for Roosevelt's acceptance of
another Progressive nomination was equivalent to
reëlecting Wilson.[34] But a majority of the Republican

delegates had already been pledged against the Colonel. They reproached him with causing the defeat of 1912, and the leaders knew also that he would not again accept the candidacy of the Progressive Party. Roosevelt understood that his own chance for obtaining the Republican nomination was vain, and, not without some difficulty, urged the Progressives to support Hughes. The greater number then returned to the Republican Party, to mark the death of the Bull Moose. Politically Roosevelt could feel that he was back at last among those with whom his triumphs in life had been associated.

A petty faction fight in California, into which Hughes stumbled innocently, changed the history of the world. Without this a Republican victory was assured, and if Hughes had been in the White House, our attitude during the peace negotiations and afterward would have been very different. Whether Roosevelt could have become President in 1916 is questionable, for the country had not yet swung far enough toward him. Regrettable as the outcome then appeared, his place in history has probably become more secure by reason of his failure to obtain the nomination. Even if he had been elected, even if he had been the magnificent War President which he would have made, his memory might not at once have become so firmly enshrined in the affection of the American people. Former rancors would have been stirred up and many might have begrudged him the third term which the country had refused to General Grant. There exists with us a curious unformulated balance between office and service. Votes cast at an election are regarded almost as settling any obligation owing to an individual for the work he has performed. If Roosevelt again in 1916 had been elevated to the Presidency, some would have found that he had received more than was his due. Instead, to the advantage of his future fame, no blemish of office came during these eventful years between him and the expression of his patriotism for the services which he alone could render.

IX

The division which Roosevelt desired to recruit and take over to France has been judged too exclusively from a purely professional military angle. The Colonel's plan was an old one which he had ruminated years before, on his Western ranch, when he hoped for some trouble to break out either with England or with Mexico in order to allow him to raise a few squadrons of cowboys. Later he had ridden this idea successfully into the White House, and it was natural that he should revert to an expanded plan which satisfied his fighting instinct, his taste for leadership, and his patriotism. Its essence was amateurish, though in keeping with the amateurish tradition which had characterized our entrance into every previous war.

It is understandable that in a great national emergency this plan should have run counter to the opinions of the Regular Army. Civil War memories of draft riots still worried the War Department, and the problem of suddenly having to train several million men raised by conscription hardly allowed for the cream of the officers to be skimmed in order to organize a fancy division. It is also understandable that General Pershing, with grave responsibilities before him, should not have welcomed a Roosevelt Division, for reasons which had nothing to do with any personal feelings he might entertain toward the Colonel. Roosevelt originally had singled out Pershing's merit in the Philippines and advanced him with quick promotion. It could only be embarrassing for the commander of a new army to have a former President and a former chief under him as his subordinate at the head of an organization of his own.

Wilson had left the full responsibility for all military matters with General Pershing, and doubtless, if the latter had recommended Roosevelt for service abroad, he would have acquiesced in this. The one interview between the President and Roosevelt was on the surface frank and friendly, and it has been said by those who knew Wilson well that he was sincerely moved by the plea of Roosevelt and sympathized with his wish for service far more than could have been expected of him.

Perhaps Wilson's stubborn fidelity to any abstract idea which he had once espoused restrained his more human feelings toward Roosevelt. In the President's Miltonic view of the Great War, personally imbued with the deep faith of which he had already made himself the prophet, he could see before him only the need for a vast scientific operation which no human sentiment should be allowed to swerve by a hair's-breadth from its harsh necessities. He was sending Pershing as his own angel of destruction to conquer the forces of evil, and whatever did not fit into the latter's plan of combat had to be ruthlessly rejected. No exception could be made, not even one for Roosevelt himself.

Did any other factors enter into his decision? As soon as one plunges into those unfathomed depths where soundings are vain, it becomes idle to ask if some furtive or unacknowledged pettier and less worthy personal feeling then impinged on the shaping of his public duty.

Although the professional reasons against the division appear convincing, it cannot be said that President Wilson's readiness to take refuge behind these, in order to explain his refusal to utilize Roosevelt in some other capacity, shows him, humanly speaking, in a generous light. At a time when four million Americans had been called for duty, there surely was room for one more. Roosevelt, it is true, was no scientific soldier, and was without experience in handling large bodies of men, but few of our officers had up to that time enjoyed this opportunity. He possessed, however, an incomparable personal prestige, resourcefulness, and the habit of command, and granted a competent staff there seems no convincing reason why he should not have been given one of the newly formed divisions in the same way that certain of these were distributed to officers of the National Guard, who later acquitted themselves with credit. Even if other causes left this undesirable, there were enough positions in the United States, either made or to be made, which he could have filled to advantage. At a time when in

Europe party lines had broken down and men of opposite political faith worked together in defense of their country, it is little to the honor of Wilson to have kept his most prominent political rival away from all participation in the Nation's effort. McKinley had shown himself more generous to Bryan during the Spanish War. Roosevelt's life had been spent in service which would have fitted him for military duty, and he had preached preparedness when Wilson still faced in a contrary direction. At the very moment when Roosevelt's ideas had finally triumphed and he could view with pride the entire country roused for action which his foresight had helped to prepare, he found himself eliminated from all participation.

The blow was cruel and its bitterness rankled. He felt with good ground that Wilson had succeeded in putting General Wood and himself on the side lines, 'and at my age the chance of my ever again taking an active part in affairs is infinitesimal.' [35] Ironically he complained, 'It is a very exclusive war.' The moral suffering he then underwent, feeling that he had no other means than to use word and pen from afar when his heart was aching to be sent to the front, enshrined him like another Napoleon as a prisoner on the rock of St. Helena.

Is it to be wondered that Roosevelt's feelings toward Wilson should have turned into bitter hatred? After our entrance into the war he was willing to admit that the Administration had done well on some points. He commended Wilson at times and praised publicly, as a great state paper, the President's Message to Congress asking for a declaration of war

against Germany. But he regarded Wilson himself as
hypocritical, rancorously partisan, and selfish. Most
of all, his accepted designation as an idealist angered
him intensely. Roosevelt was unable to appreciate
the finer sides of Wilson or soar with him toward
these astral heights where, in a realm of pure ideas
floating in space, the latter could pursue his sincere
dreams for ameliorating the lot of humanity. The
term 'ideals' has become so hackneyed in our common verbiage that often it covers the lack of inward
substance. The avenues which lead to the domain of
ideals also reveal less noble perspectives, and Roosevelt scoffed at the abuse of ethical terminology by
Wilson till he saw in his altruistic doctrine nothing
more than the latter's partisan side grasping at personal power.

No two men could have been more different than
Roosevelt and Wilson in their superficial tastes, as
well as in origin, environment, training, and phrase-
ology. Almost the only point of resemblance appeared in their mutual dislike. Yet in a curious way,
professing contradictory opinions on most subjects,
both men possessed not a few points of similarity.
Both had a genius for phrases, the one picturesque
and popular in appeal, the other vague under an
apparent precision, but suggestive and stimulating.
Both were fond of wide, though not always deep,
reading. Both were intensely partisan and personal,
avid for power, and ready like most great leaders to
sacrifice men to a desired accomplishment. Both were
lifted by high ambition which took a purely practical
and political view of the means to attain their goals,

and both preferred to use short cuts and irregular methods, which often astonished the observer, rather than to restrict themselves to more normal processes. Both also in the loftier reaches of their vision disregarded all other considerations, even those urged by their better judgment, in order to try to achieve the end in view. And both, whatever motives of selfish purpose guided their original action, were able on occasion to soar beyond these and attain an elevation in which egotism was left standing at the outer door. Both, too, in the end suffered a similar fate. After early years of struggle, both suddenly had been raised to the highest eminence of mortal man, and both with equal suddenness were hurled down from their peak into solitude and impotence. The pity lay that there was no room under our one-man system for Roosevelt and Wilson, and that the harsh reactions of power in American democracy tend so completely to exclude those who do not partake of its favors.

Roosevelt gave his support to Wilson's war measures. He made addresses in the West on 'Americanism and War.' He spoke often in training camps. His four sons went to France, two to be wounded and one to meet his death fighting in the air. Like a Roman father, on the day he learned this, Roosevelt proceeded to Saratoga to deliver the speech he had promised to make. He merely stated that 'Quentin's mother and I are very glad that he got to the front and had a chance to render some service to his country and to show the stuff there was in him before his fate befel him' — words which will be impressive to all time in the quiet dignity of their patriotism. Later, he wrote that life and death formed part of the same great adventure, and only those are fit to live who do not fear to die, remarking that the inspiration for his thought came from Quentin. To an afflicted friend he wrote that it was idle to rail at the inevitable, for 'serene and high of heart, we must face our fate and go down into the darkness.'

In the summer of 1918, Roosevelt was approached by men who hitherto had been his bitterest adversaries, soliciting him to be the Republican candidate for Governor of New York. Barnes himself issued a public statement that he favored his candidacy. But Roosevelt refused on the ground that his mind was then absorbed with considering the great problems of the war and that he could not abandon these for State issues. His thoughts were with his boys in France, with his own silent grief, and with the Nation's attitude toward the war and what would come afterward. Even the Presidency in 1920 seemed a paltry thing. He declared that he was indifferent to it nor would he lift a finger to get it. Occasionally the feeling swept over him that he was no longer the man required for the situation. At Saratoga, in the summer of 1918, he remarked to a prominent New York politician that he did not understand the United States of 1920 and that he had ceased to be the man best fitted for the Presidency. The America he knew was the country which he had been able to lead in the early years of the century. Great new forces had arisen, almost anonymous in their expression and beyond his comprehension. Instinctively he felt that the Nation had gone outside his reach. There was in our life an economic equivalent for the Unknown Warrior, which escaped his understanding.

Undoubtedly he would have been the Republican candidate in 1920. Undoubtedly, too, he would have been elected at least by the same overwhelming majority that put Harding into office. He would have thrown himself into the campaign with the same zest as before and already he was giving thought to the men he wanted to surround him. He would have found once more that the country needed him in shaping its new destinies.

It is idle to speculate about the trend which American history would have taken had he become President. The people acclaimed him as the next leader, but Fate willed otherwise. His health had been undermined by illness and he had been weighted down by grief for his dead son. The volcano inside him had broken down the human frame of the Titan and death overtook him peacefully in his sleep on the sixth of January, 1919. He too was a victim of the Great War.

EPILOGUE

RIGHTLY Roosevelt stands enshrined in the same company as our two greatest Presidents. The country sees in him a national hero in whom every American can feel pride. Already a half-legendary Roosevelt is being woven into the Nation's imagination.

There was something universal in the different elements which formed his soul. Mr. Jusserand has aptly likened him to radium from which emanated an energy which infused all around him. There are traces in him of the Roman whom Plutarch would have delighted to describe, the Elizabethan worthy, the pilgrim, the eighteenth-century squire, and the Western pioneer, all leading up to form the twentieth-century American. In his tastes as in his origin he regarded himself as a kind of synthesis of the United States and deliberately shaped his life in that direction. No American lives who cannot see some side of himself, some trait or inward aspiration, exemplified in Roosevelt. Sparks from the fire of his soul were spread among millions. In this lay the touch of his genius. Generations to come will feel that the Nation has been enriched by his life, and like a hero of ancient days it can be said of him that he deserved well of his country.

NOTES

CHAPTER I

1. Letter to Mrs. Cowles, August 22, 1880.
2. J. B. Bishop, *Theodore Roosevelt and His Time, Shown in His Letters*, I, 18.
3. Bishop, I, 19.
4. *Autobiography*, 81.
5. September 20, 1884.
6. August 20, 1886.
7. Letter to Lodge, March 27, 1886.
8. June 7, 1886.
9. Letter to Lodge, October 17, 1886.
10. Letter to Lodge, October 20, 1886.
11. November 1, 1886.
12. January 6, 1887.
13. Letter to Lodge, March 7, 1887.
14. Letter to Mrs. Cowles, January 6, 1887.
15. April 20, 1887.
16. C. R. Robinson: *My Brother Theodore Roosevelt*, 137–38.
17. Letter to Lodge, March 25, 1889.
18. August 22, 1888.
19. August 20, 1887.
20. July 1, 1889.
21. June 24, 1889.
22. Letter to Lodge, October 11, 1894.
23. Letter to Mrs. Cowles, February 11, 1894.
24. Letter to Mrs. Cowles, April 10, 1890.
25. Letter to Lodge, July 22, 1891.
26. Letter to Mrs. Cowles, May 27, 1894.
27. Letter to Mrs. Cowles, December 17, 1893.
28. Letter of May 19, 1895.
29. Letter of August 3, 1895.
30. Letter to Mrs. Cowles, June 30, 1895.
31. Letter to Mrs. Cowles, June 23, 1895.
32. Letter to Mrs. Cowles, February 25, 1896.
33. Letter to Mrs. Cowles, January 26, 1896.
34. Letter of September 22, 1895.
35. Letter to Lodge, October 11, 1895.
36. Bishop, I, 68.

37. Letter to Lodge, December 20, 1895.
38. December 27, 1895.
39. January 19, 1896.
40. Letter to Mrs. Cowles, March 9, 1896.
41. Letter to Mrs. Cowles, April 5, 1896.
42. October 16, 1897.
43. Letter to Mrs. Cowles, March 30, 1896.
44. Letter to Mrs. Cowles, February 28, 1897.
45. Letter to Lodge, September 21, 1897.
46. October 5, 1897.
47. Bishop, I, 102, 103.
48. July 5, 1898.
49. July 31, 1898.
50. December 11, 1899.
51. Page 285.
52. Letter to Mrs. Cowles, February 27, 1900.
53. Letter of December 7, 1899.
54. Letter to Edward S. Martin, November 22, 1900; Bishop, I, 140.
55. Letter to Lodge, August 20, 1901.

CHAPTER II

1. Bishop, II, 94.
2. Bishop, I, 166.
3. J. Hampton Moore, *Roosevelt and the Old Guard*, 221.
4. Letter to Lodge, July 30, 1896.
5. Bishop, I, 279.
6. Bishop, I, 308.
7. Roosevelt to Spring Rice, December 27, 1904; *The Letters and Friendships of Sir Cecil Spring Rice*, I, 442, seq.
8. *Ibid.*, I, 470.
9. Roosevelt to Spring Rice, December 27, 1904; *Spring Rice*, I, 442.
10. Roosevelt to Spring Rice, July 24, 1905; *Spring Rice*, I, 478.
11. Roosevelt to Spring Rice, June 13, 1904; *Spring Rice*, I, 418.
12. Bishop, I, 401.
13. Letter to Lodge, May 15, 1905.
14. April 7, 1907.
15. Quoted in L. Abbott: *Impressions of T. R.*, p. 66.

CHAPTER III

1. July 19, 1908.
2. July 26, 1909.

3. Letter to Lodge, September 10, 1909

4. January 15, 1910.

5. Bishop, II, 211.

6. Bishop, II, 203.

7. O. K. Davis: *Released for Publication*, 200. [Invaluable for its account of the Progressive Campaign.]

8. Davis, 204.

9. October 21, 1910. Bishop, II, 306.

10. Davis, 223.

11. Davis, 279, *et seq.*

12. Davis, 295, *seq.*

13. Davis, 305, *seq.*

14. W. R. Thayer, *Roosevelt*, 353, *et seq.*

15. Davis, 382.

16. Davis, 387.

17. Bishop, II, 343.

18. Letter to Kermit Roosevelt, January 27, 1915; Bishop, II, 358.

19. Letter to Sir Henry Lucy, December 18, 1912; Bishop, II, 348.

20. Letter to W. A. White, November 7, 1914; Bishop, II, 355.

21. Letter to Kermit Roosevelt, January 27, 1915; Bishop, II, 358.

22. Letter to Hiram Johnson, November 9, 1914; Bishop, II, 355.

23. Davis, 434.

24. Davis, 437; letter to Lodge, February 4, 1916.

25. Letter of October 3, 1914; Bishop, II, 372.

26. Letter to Lodge, December 8, 1914.

27. This article, which appeared in the *National Review* of London, in November, 1914, along with another prophesying the war, to which allusion has already been made, was later published, with an introduction by Theodore Roosevelt, under the title of *A Prophecy of the War*, by the Columbia University Press, in 1917.

28. August 7, 1915; Bishop, II, 392.

29. See Appendix for copy of a letter addressed to the writer, dated February 19, 1915.

30. December 8, 1914.

31. Letter to Lodge, November 27, 1915.

32. Letter to George W. Perkins, September 3, 1915; Bishop, II, 397.

33. Letter to Lodge, January 26, 1916.

34. Davis, 448.

35. Letter to Lodge, May 26, 1917.

APPENDIX

THEODORE ROOSEVELT

THIRTY EAST FORTY-SECOND STREET
NEW YORK CITY, *February* 19, 1915

MY DEAR MR. EINSTEIN:

I was much interested in your article on 'American Peace Dreams.' But you must pardon my saying that I do not think you do justice to me when you only quote what I said about my plan for peace. Taft, Wilson, and Bryan stand on an absolutely and completely different footing from me in this matter, because they explicitly or implicitly propose to substitute paper agreements for the potential use of force and explicitly or implicitly treat these proposed paper agreements as reasons why America should not prepare to defend itself. Moreover, they treat their proposals as being immediately realizable, as offering immediate substitutes for war; and, what is to my mind most important of all and fundamentally utterly immoral, they dare not say one word for righteousness, but advocate peace in terms that would consecrate wrong. My proposal was a wholly subordinate part of the lesson I was teaching. I hope you have seen the little book in which it appeared, called 'America and the World War.' I explicitly stated that a world league for peace is not now in sight; that it may never be created, and that at present the prime necessity is that our Nation shall be able to defend by its own strength its honor and its vital interest; and that this is the most important lesson taught the United States by the present war. I wish to make good people who abhor unjust war feel, as I myself sincerely feel, that the men who think as I do not offer strength or force as the only permanent solution of international questions, that we believe it should be combined with righteousness, with fair dealing. I desire to hold this up as an ideal, a possibly realizable ideal. I do this both because I believe in the ideal and because I believe, furthermore, that by making good citizens understand that this is genuinely our ideal, we can also make them go with us in the immediately and vitally important part of our policy, which is preparation to use our own strength to defend our own rights. Now, if you will look at my book I think you will see that Messrs. Wilson, Bryan, and Taft stand at the absolutely opposite pole from me. For example, I emphatically do mean that we should not sign Hague Conventions with European Powers unless we are willing by the use of force to try to make those conventions effective in just such a case as that of Belgium. As regards America, I was very careful to limit the number of nations as to which such a court would be applicable. It would be pure damage to establish in this hemisphere such a court so far as the affairs of Mexico, of most of the Central American and of most of the northern South American states are concerned.

In other words, my dear Mr. Einstein, I was just a little bit disappointed that you, with your admirable historic sense, should fail to see that Messrs. Wilson, Bryan, and Taft propose immediate remedies which are false and mischievous, because they make no effort whatever to provide for keeping promises and because they treat the making of foolish promises as a substitute for efficient preparation on our part; whereas my ground is that no promise is to be made unless it is to be kept; that no promise is worth anything unless there is a method of enforcing it; and that as things are at present it is criminal for a nation to blind itself to actual facts and to fail to prepare to defend itself with its own strength.

In what I have been doing I have not been acting in
the interest of England as such or against the interest of
Germany as such; I have been acting in the interest of
the United States and also in accordance with what I
believe to be our duty of judging each nation by its
conduct in any given case. I should do this in any
event....

Faithfully yours

(Signed)   THEODORE ROOSEVELT

HON. LEWIS EINSTEIN

INDEX

INDEX

259

Roosevelt, 64; Roosevelt to, 146; Roosevelt's later attitude toward, 165; selected as candidate for the Presidency, 170–72; his Administration, 178, 192; his relations with Roosevelt, 186–88, 193–97; and the 1912 election, 196, 199, 206

Tammany Hall, 17–19; Roosevelt learned much from, 17, 18; personal contact of friendship and service in, 17, 19; and reformers, 19

Tariff, the, 45

Tariff Board, 192

Taxation of public franchises, 82

Taylor, Admiral, 66

Thayer, William Roscoe, 210

Trevelyan, Sir George, 41, 180; letter of Roosevelt to, 95

Trusts, 154–57, 159–62

Turkey, relations with United States, 134

Unions, labor, 152

Van Buren, Martin, 77

Van Roosevelt, Klaes Martensen, Roosevelt's first American ancestor, 3

Varilla, Philippe Bunau, interview with Roosevelt, 124

Venezuela, affair of, under Cleveland, 60, 71, 128; affair of, under Roosevelt, 128–30

Wainwright, Richard, 66

Wall Street, 118

Washburn, Charles S., 101

Washington, D.C., society of, 50–52; simplicity of life in, 51; beautified by Roosevelt, 91, 92

Washington, Booker, invited to the White House, 106

Washington, George, 175

White, Henry, American Ambassador to Italy, delegate to Algeciras Conference, 145

White, Stanford, plans Government buildings at Washington, 92

'White man's burden,' 122, 182

William II, German Emperor, accepts arbitration over Venezuela, 129, 130; Roosevelt's opinion of, 142; and the Algeciras Conference, 143–47; letter of Roosevelt to, 173

Wilson, Woodrow, essays the popular appeal, 78; recommends compensation for Colombia, 121; his peace plan, 222; Roosevelt's opinion of, 226–28, 238, 239; his 'too proud to fight' speech, 227; his interview with Roosevelt, 236; as regards his refusal to give Roosevelt a commission, 236–38; compared with Roosevelt, 239; preaches neutrality, 225

Wolcott, 64

Wood, Gen. Leonard, 71, 238

World War, 222–42